NAKED IN THE MENAGERIE

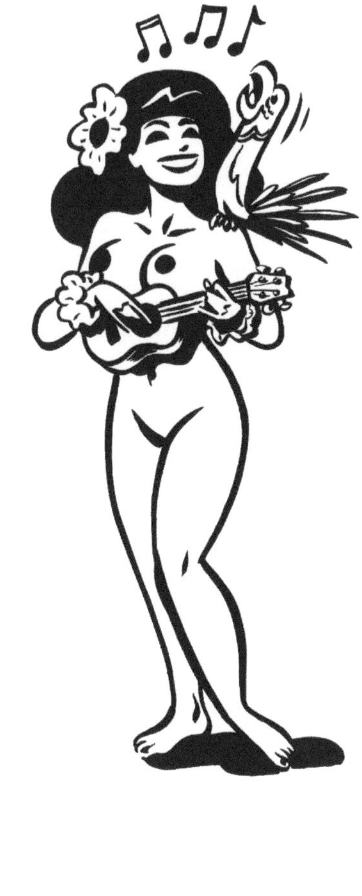

Published in 2018 by Wolfbait Books

ISBN: 9781999744175

A catalogue record of this book is available at The British Library.

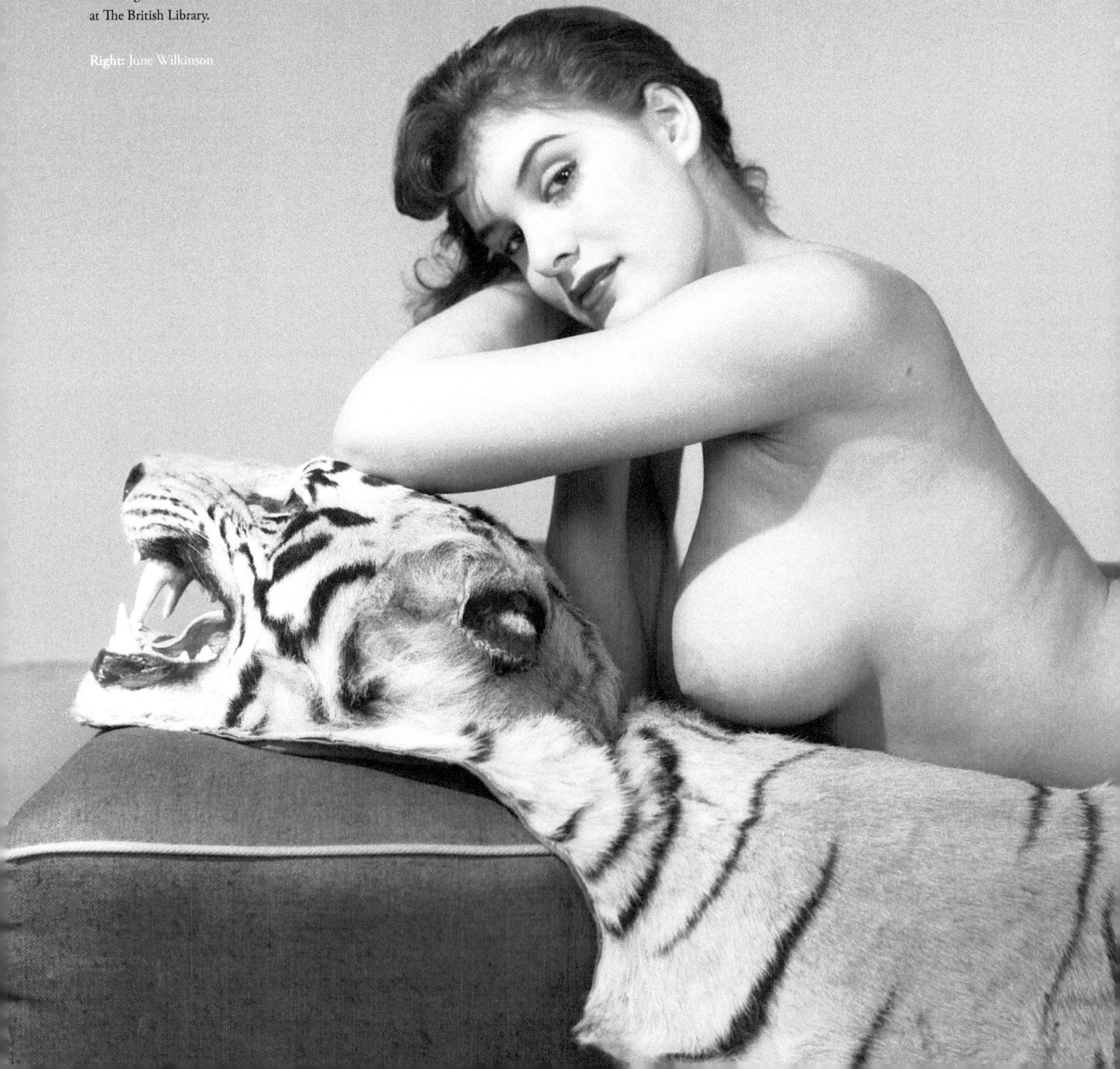

Right: June Wilkinson

NAKED IN THE MENAGERIE

By Yahya El-Droubie
Photography by Stephen Glass
Illustrations by Colin Gordon

WOLFBAIT
UNDER THE COUNTER CULTURE

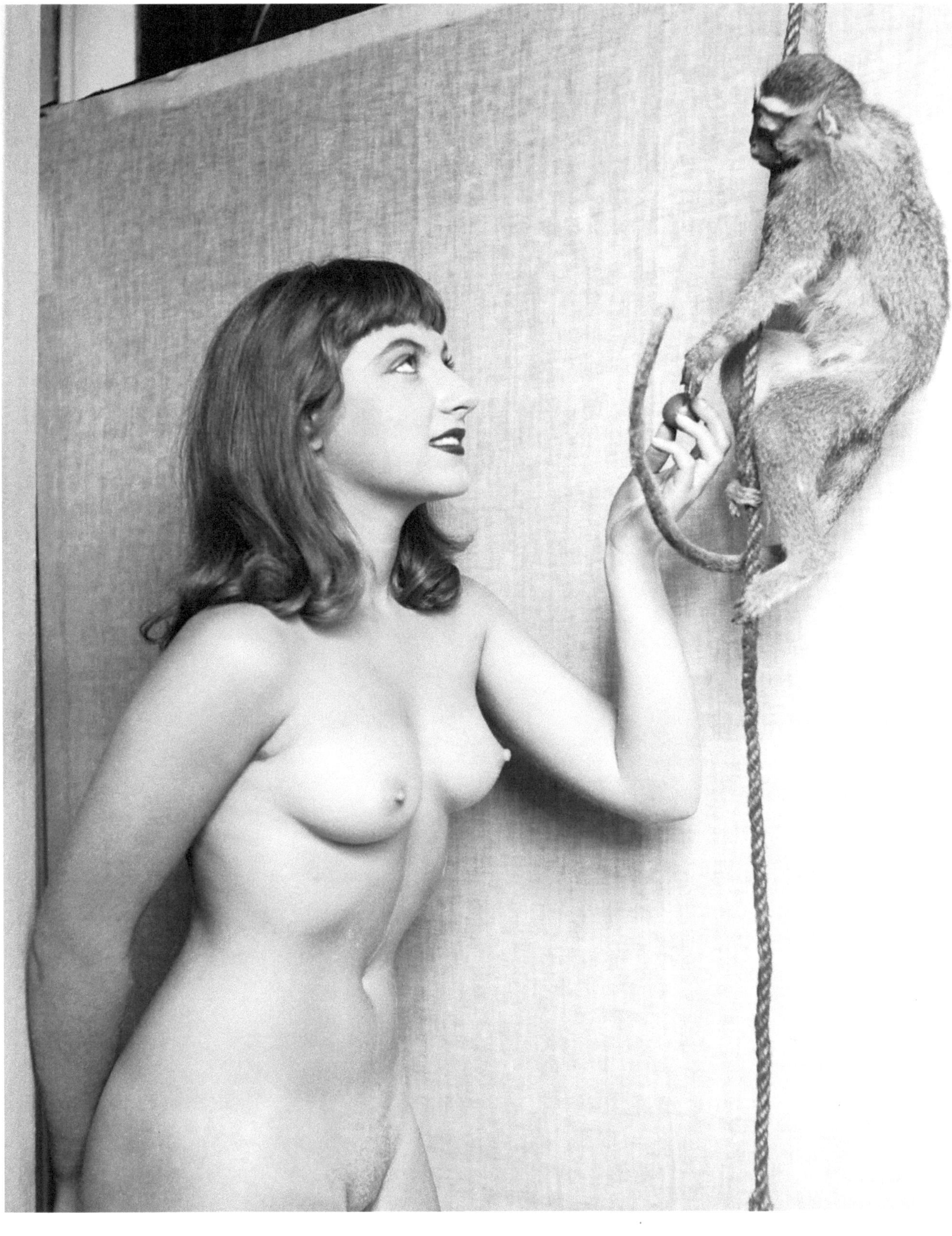

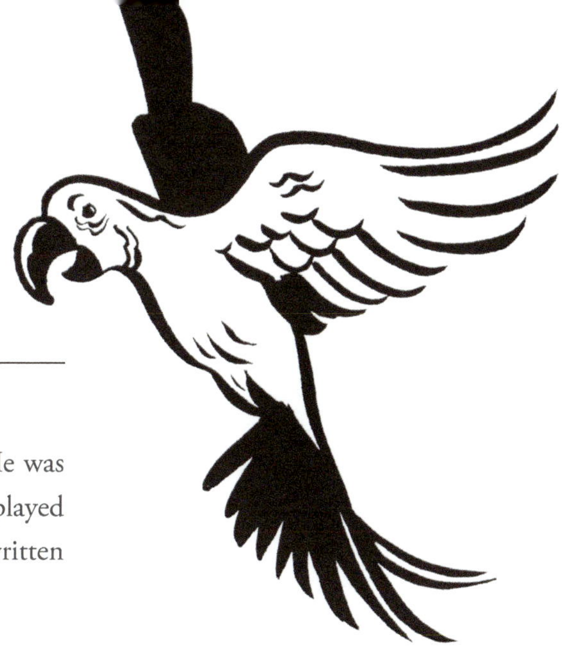

Introduction

THE PHOTOGRAPHER STEPHEN GLASS is a bit of an enigma. He was well-known enough during the 1950s for his name to be prominently displayed on the front of magazines to help sell them, but very little actually was written about him or his work.

This situation differs somewhat from that of his elder brother, Zoltán Glass, who was also a photographer. Known to his friends as "Zolly" he was featured and interviewed in numerous magazines on both sides of the Atlantic.

Zoltán was born in Budapest on April 26, 1903. He began his career as a cartoonist and retoucher for a local newspaper, but in 1925 he moved to Berlin, where he found regular employment as the picture editor of a Berlin evening paper, before moving on to the *Berliner Tagblatt* as a photojournalist. He prospered and was soon able to develop a thriving freelance business as a commercial photographer and journalist. He established Reclaphot, a photographic agency that specialised in advertising work, and Autophot, a company dedicated exclusively to automobile photography. He was an amateur racer and keen motorsport enthusiast, and he covered Germany's biggest races at the Nurburgring and the Avus circuit, near Berlin. His most famous photos are of the Mercedes-Benz Silver Arrows team, which dominated Grand Prix racing in the mid-1930s. With the rise of Hitler, however, business became increasingly difficult, and he fled to London. As an enemy alien at the outbreak of World War II, he was not permitted to pursue his profession and faced the threat of internment, so he voluntarily handed over his camera equipment to the British authorities.

After the war, he eked out a living taking publicity stills for clients in the film and theatrical worlds. His career took a big step up when the Hungarian Arpad Elfer who was Creative Director of Colman, Prentis & Varley, one of the most prestigious London ad agencies started giving him work. By the mid-Fifties, he was one of the most successful fashion and advertising photographers in London

Sir Thomas More invented an imaginary island, which he named Utopia, meaning 'nowhere' to explain his idea of what a perfect world should be like. In this too imperfect age, we could all do with occasionnal glimpses of perfect beauty such as the camera has secured in these pages.

– Benson Herbert

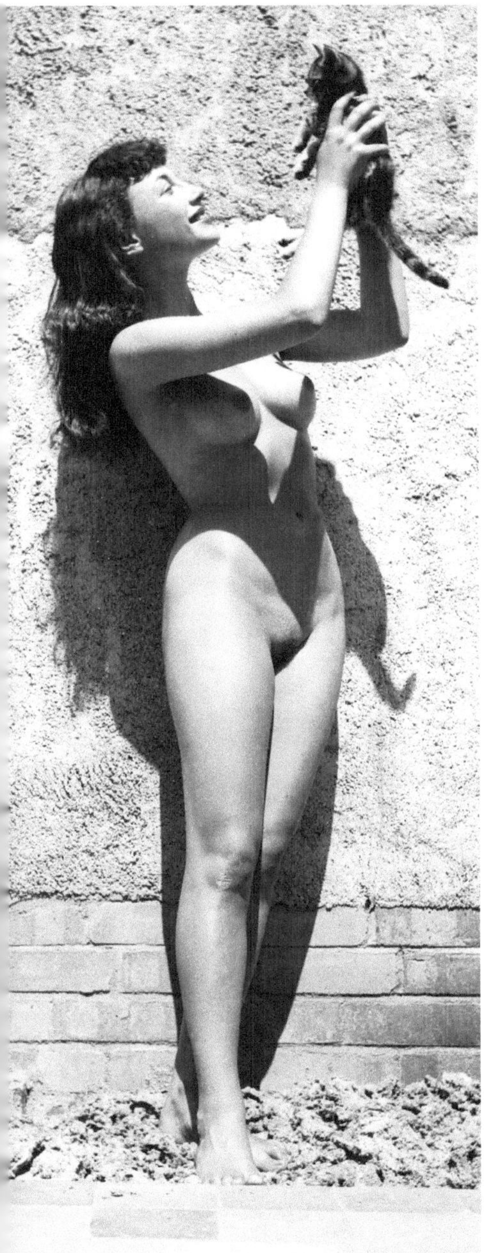

with his own studios at 183 Kings Road, Chelsea, and later at 41 Paradise Walk, SW3. One of his clients was Odhams Press who published *Lilliput*, a pocket-sized gentleman's magazine that featured an assortment of titillating articles and risqué humour, together with adventurous photographic essays from such well-known talents as Bill Brandt and Brassai.

His brother Stephen, who also fled Europe due to the Second World War, carved out a name for himself taking pictures for such publications as *The Naturist* and *Health and Efficiency.*

The well-known Pamela Green (1929-2010) modelled for him several times at the infamous nudist camp Spielplatz in Bricket Wood and at his tiny first-floor studio in Old Church Street, just of the Kings Road in Chelsea. *"In those days, when Stephen photographed me, I still had dark hair. He liked his props, especially stuffed animals."* It was Pamela's agent Pearl Beresford, who sent her along to his brother, Zoltán, whose studio on the Kings Road was enormous by comparison. Unlike Stephen, Zoltán was brisk and businesslike.

Iseult, the daughter of Charles Macaskie, the founder of Spielplatz, remembers Stephen. *"He would often ask me to pose for him. I quite enjoyed having my photo taken, but when I asked to be paid he stopped using me. A bit of pocket money back then would have been nice."*

In addition to magazines, his work graced a series of small books published by *The Naturist* such as *Sussex Maidens* (1949), *Pool of Enchantment* (1950) and *Nudist Life in Spielplatz* (1956). He also photographed the popular model June Palmer (1940-2004).

Right: Pamela Green holding a kitten (not stuffed). Taken in early 1950s.

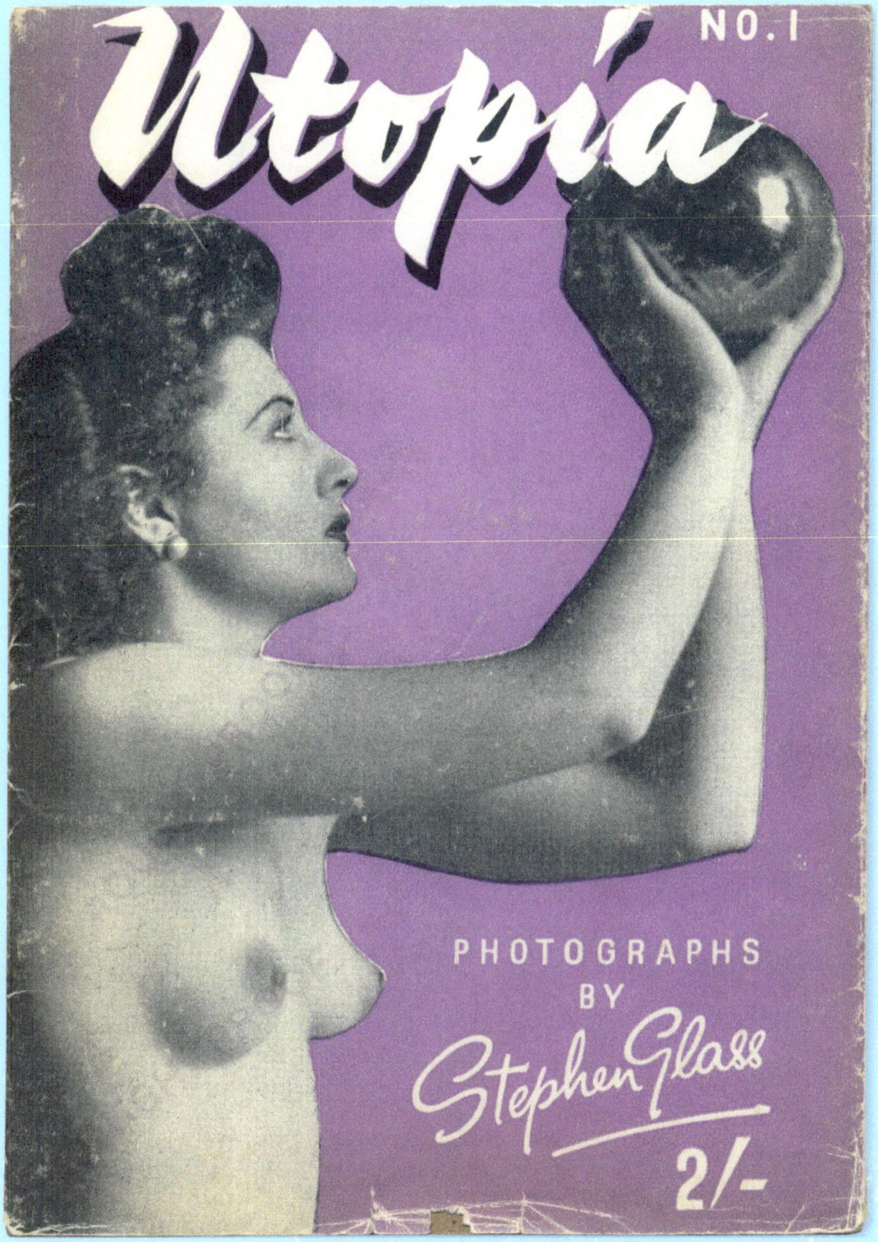

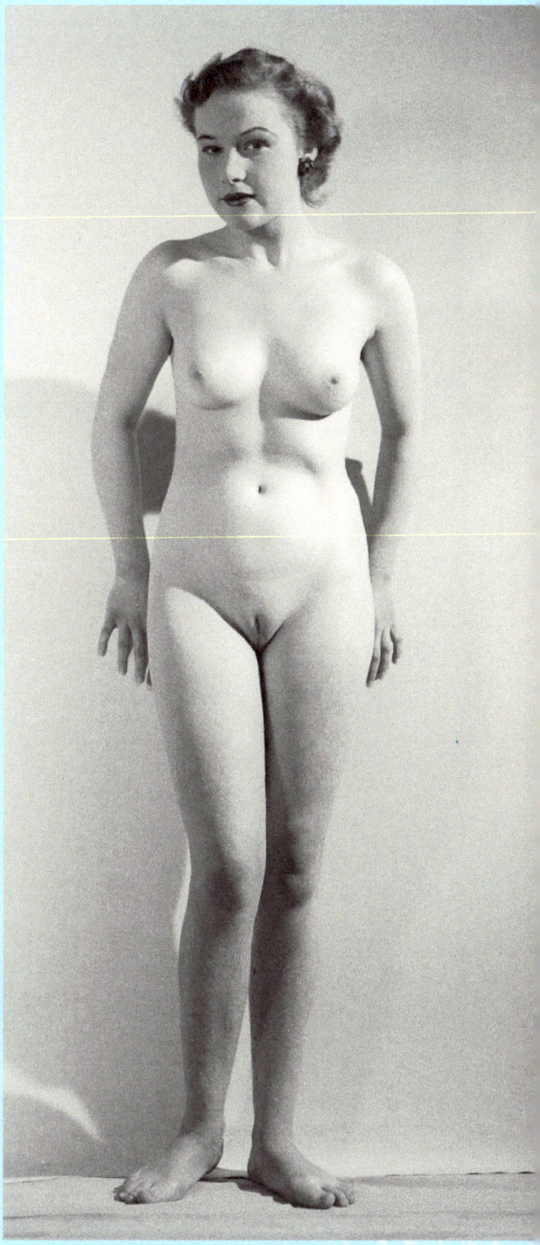

Above: *Utopia*, No. 1, a 16-page booklet with a cardboard cover. Date unknown, but probably mid-1950s. Apparently a magazine for connoisseurs and "in response to countless requests, the first of a new series of art photographs… exclusive selection of models, first-grade photography and the finest reproduction… quality not sacrificed to quantity". Published by Utopian Publications Ltd., Gloucester Mansions, Cambridge Circus, London.

Right: Studio nude probably taken in the late 1940s/early 1950s. Model: Claudia Grey.

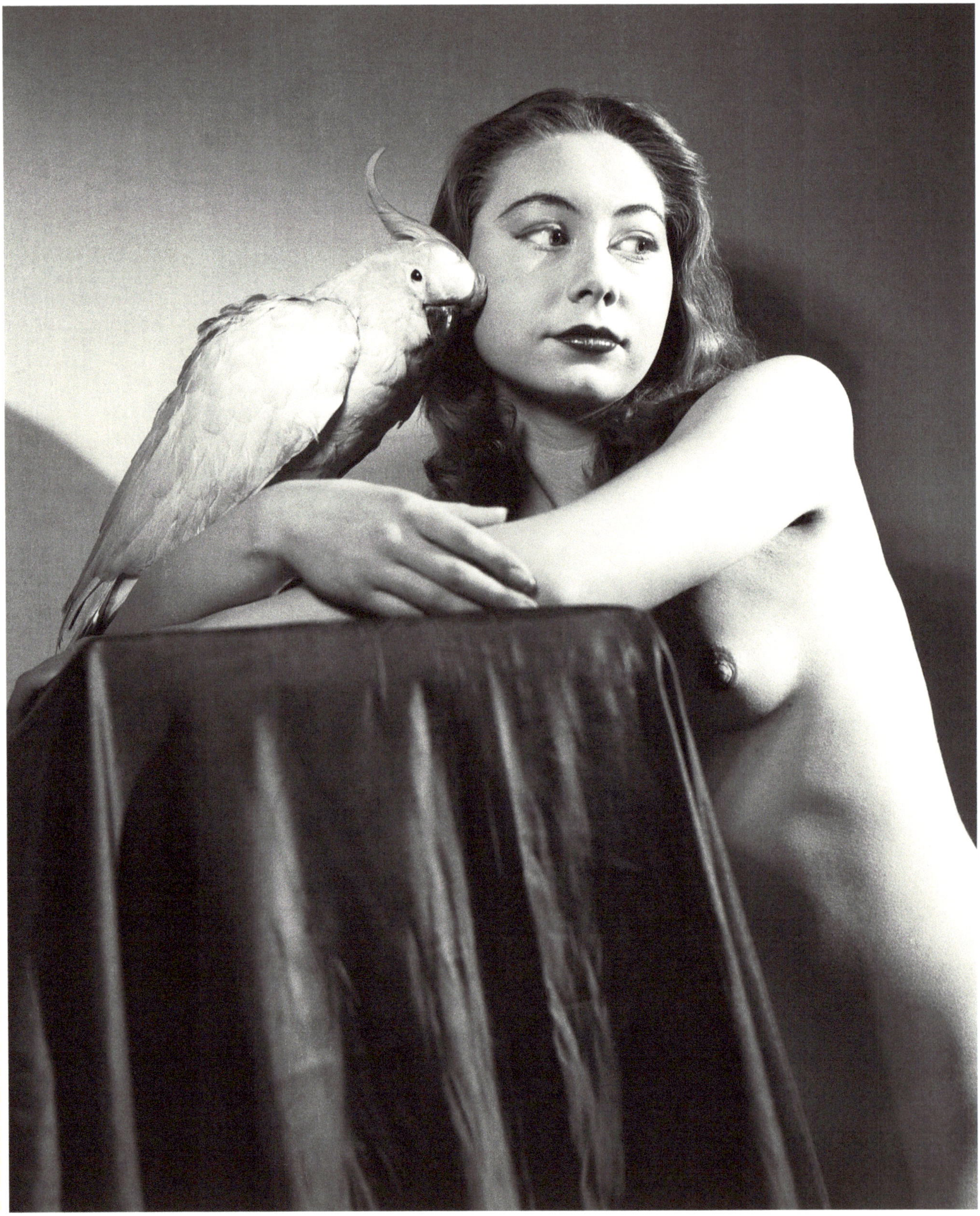

The photos in this book are from the uncensored negatives. Up to and until the end of the 1960s the showing of pubic hair or genitalia was considered obscene in Britain. To ensure a photograph of a naked young lady was suitable for publication and did not incur the wrath of the censor, a model would shave down below, and the image would be retouched by hand to erase anything problematic.

In 1964 Zoltán Glass had made enough money to sell his Chelsea studio to a consortium of British photographers and move abroad to a villa in Roquebrune on the French Riviera with his common-law wife Pat, a former cabaret dancer. He offered his collection of pin-up photography to Harrison Marks, who strangely turned him down. He died in France on February 24, 1981, at the age of 78, leaving neither offspring nor a will. His photographs were eventually left to the The National Science and Media Museum in Bradford. Stephen Glass died on 23 April 1990. His work ended up at auction.

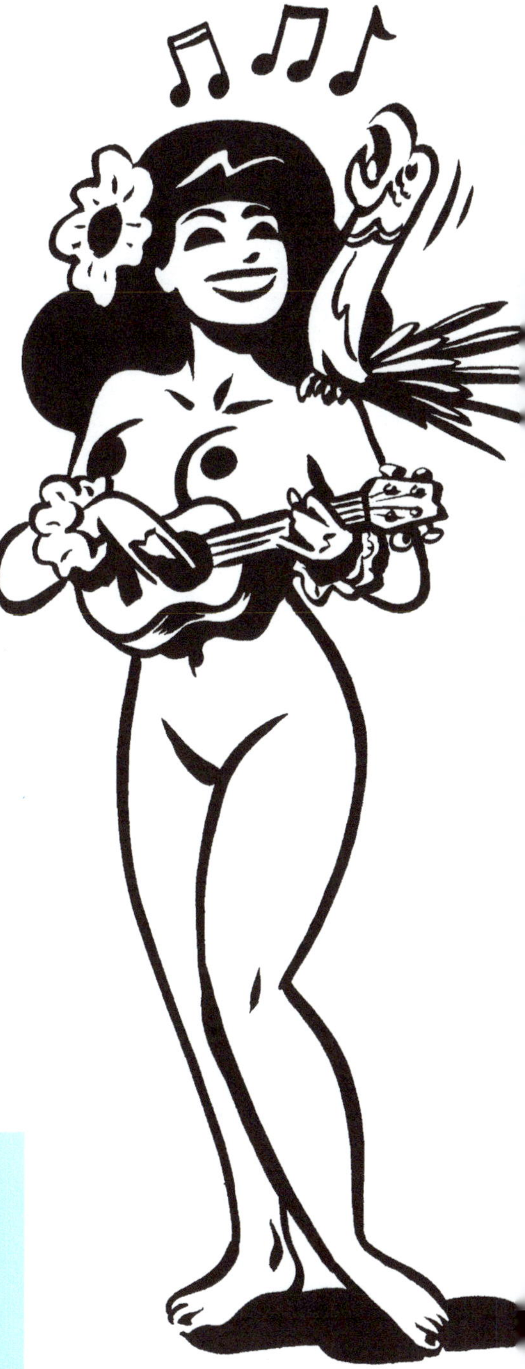

To modern eyes models posing nude with stuffed animals is a little peculiar if not downright strange. No doubt a reflection of the declining acceptance of taxidermy since the War. The images themselves, however, are part of a long tradition from Eve in the garden of Eden to Walt Disney's Snow White — innocence and nature in mythological harmony. What's not to like?

The bulk of the indoor photographs were probably taken in Stephen's flat at 60 Old Church Street, less than a ten-minute walk from his brother's studio on the Kings Road, London. Other locations include Spielplatz, a naturist village in Bricketwood near St. Albans, Hertfordshire, England. The photos of the ever-delightful Pamela Green on pages 42 and 43 were taken there. Charles Macaskie founded the village in 1929. His daughter Iseult still lives there to this very day.

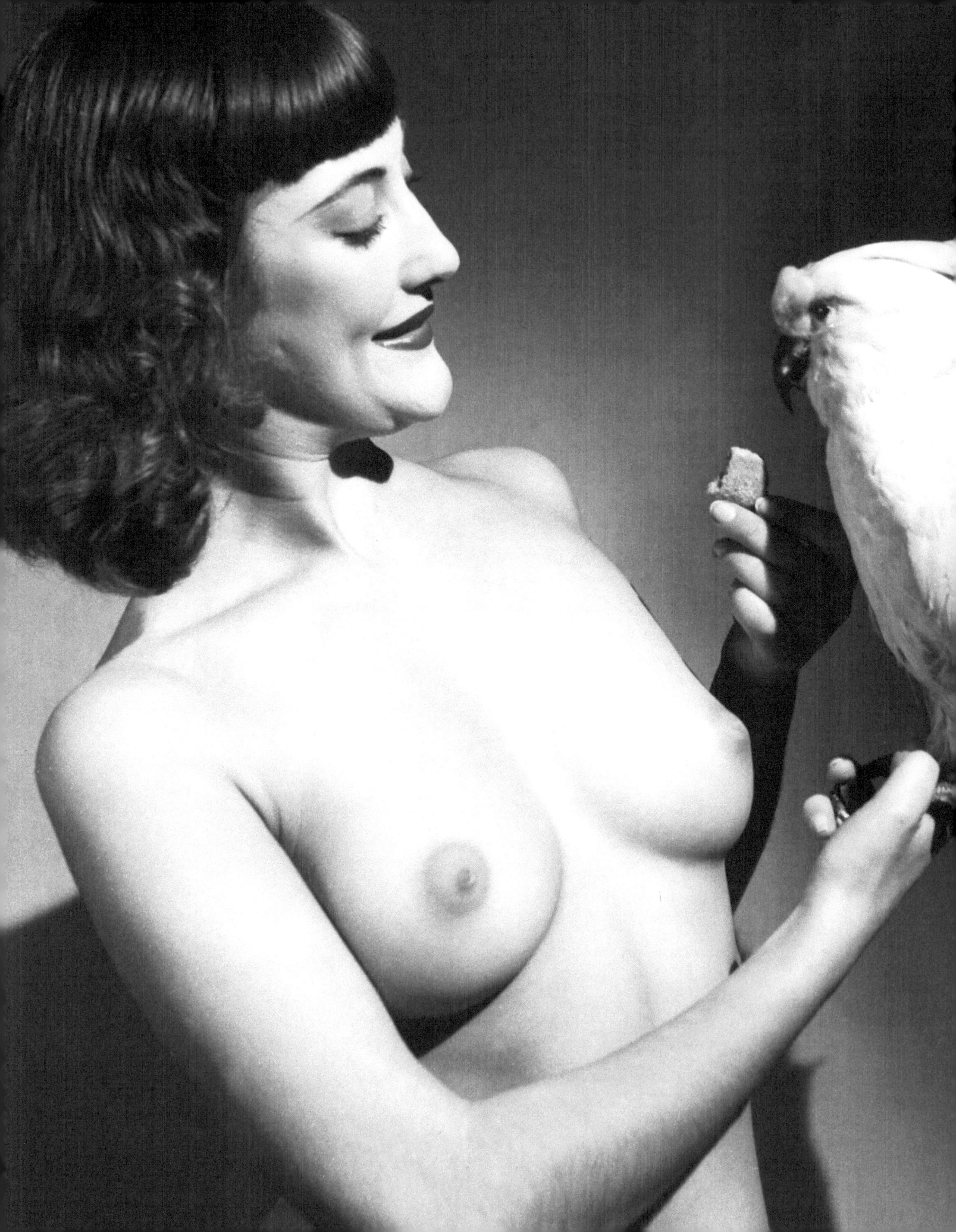

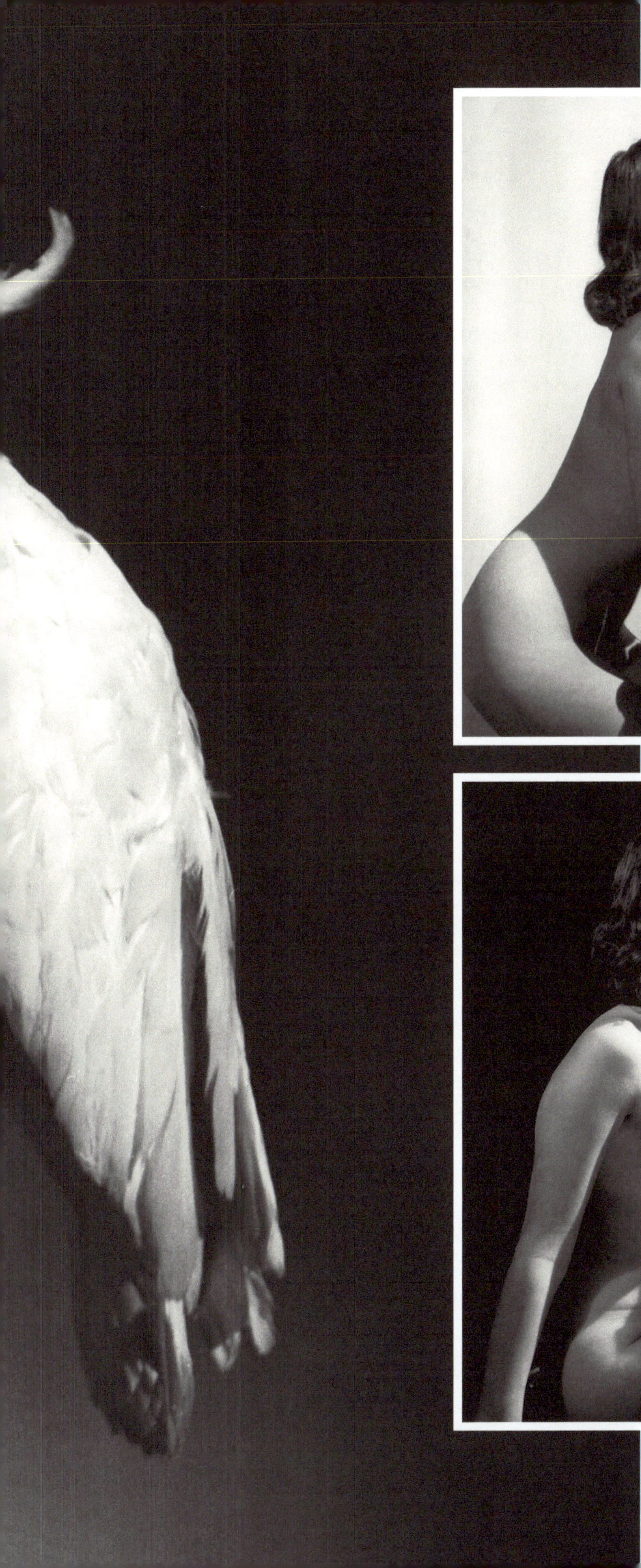
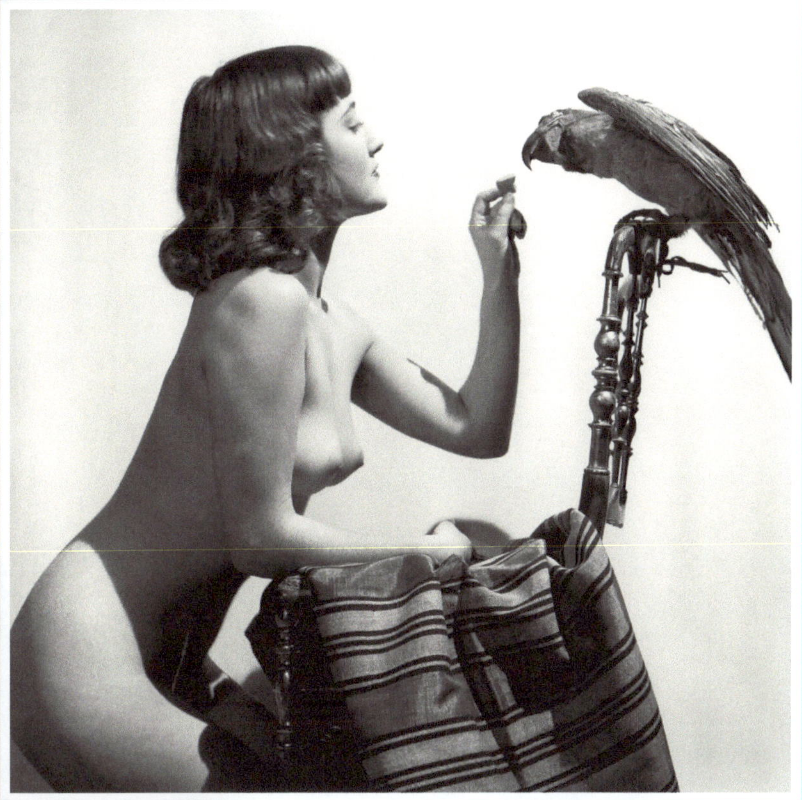
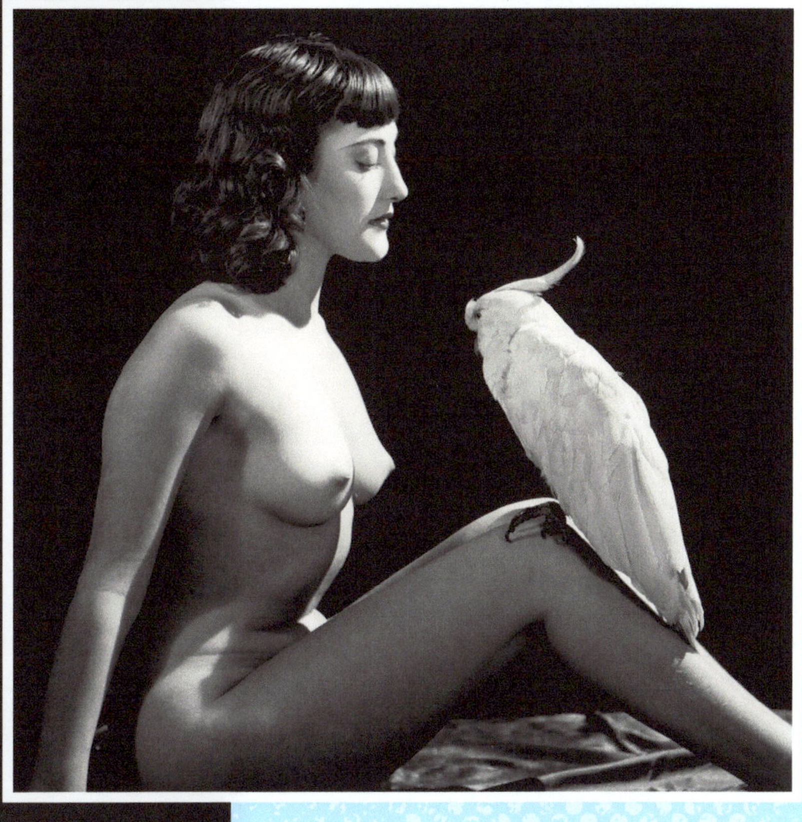

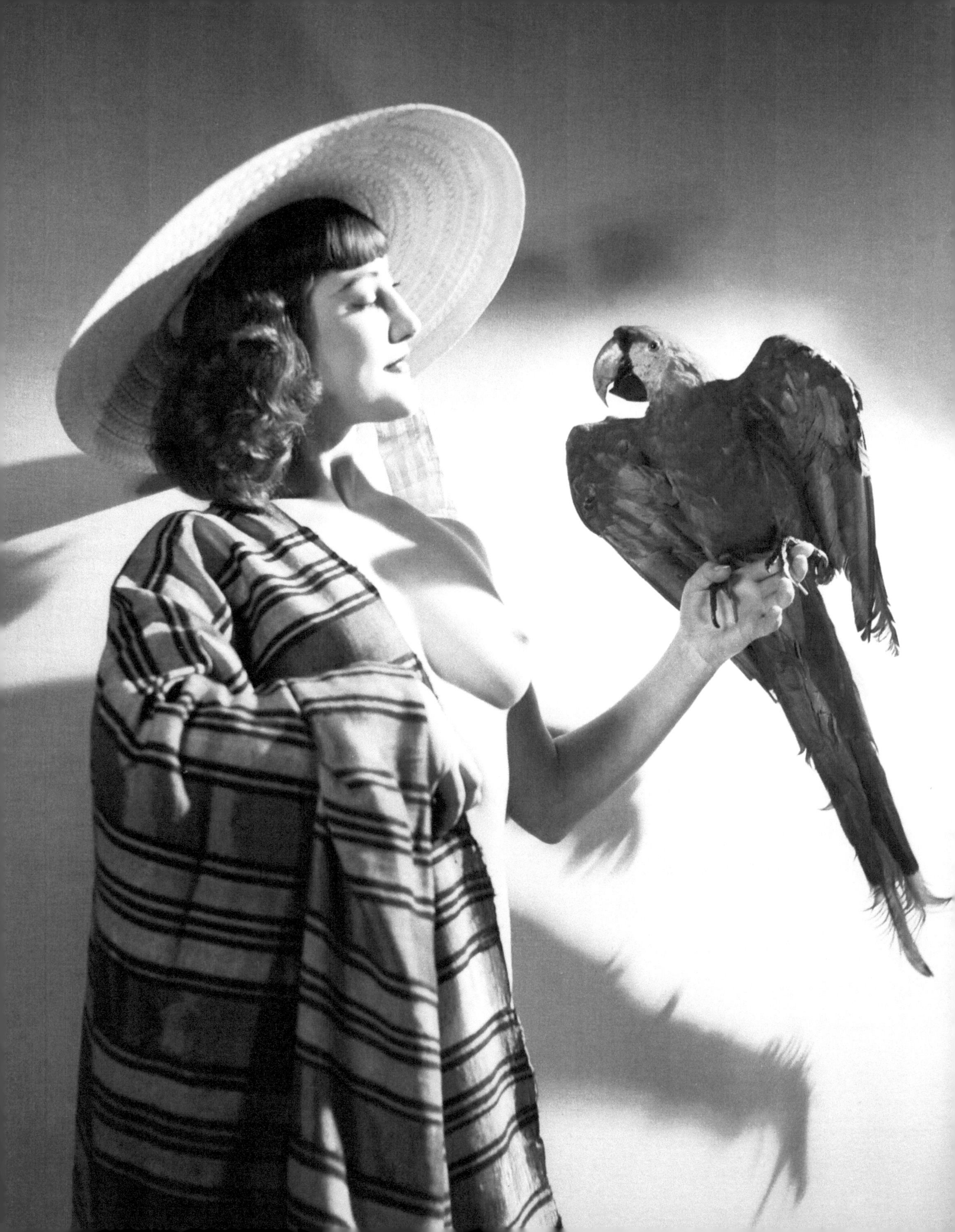

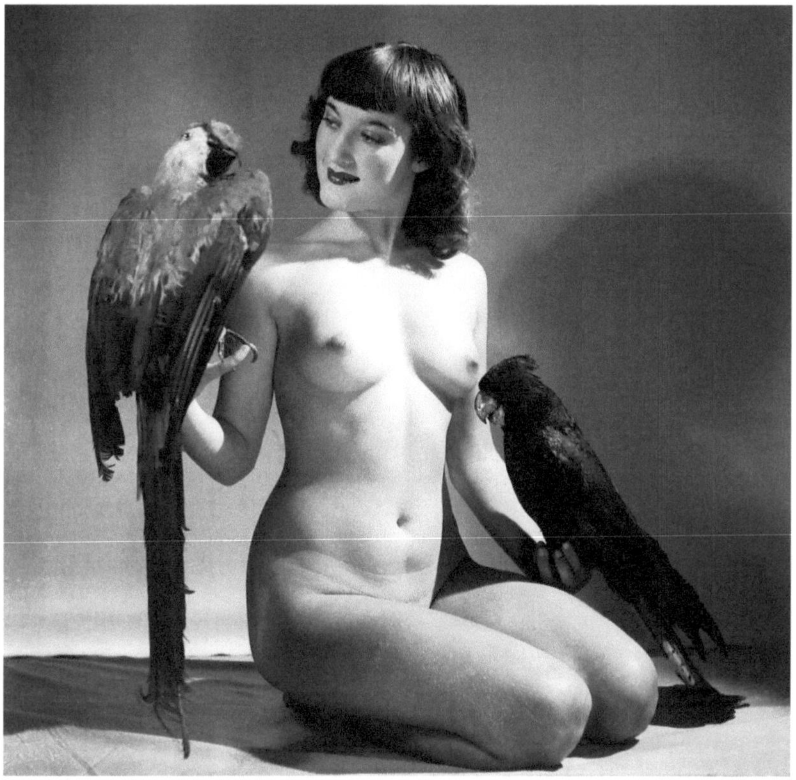

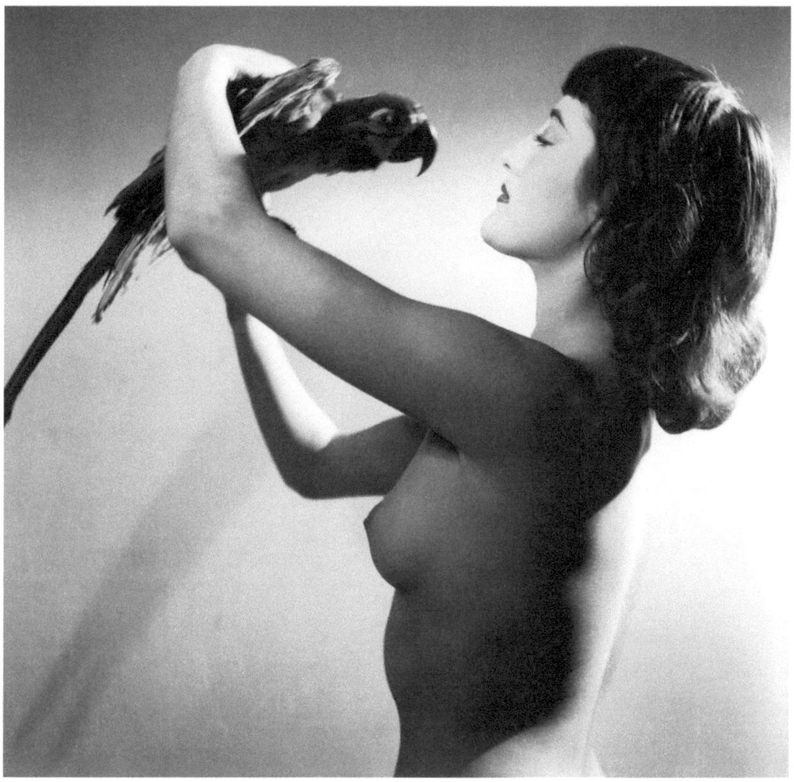

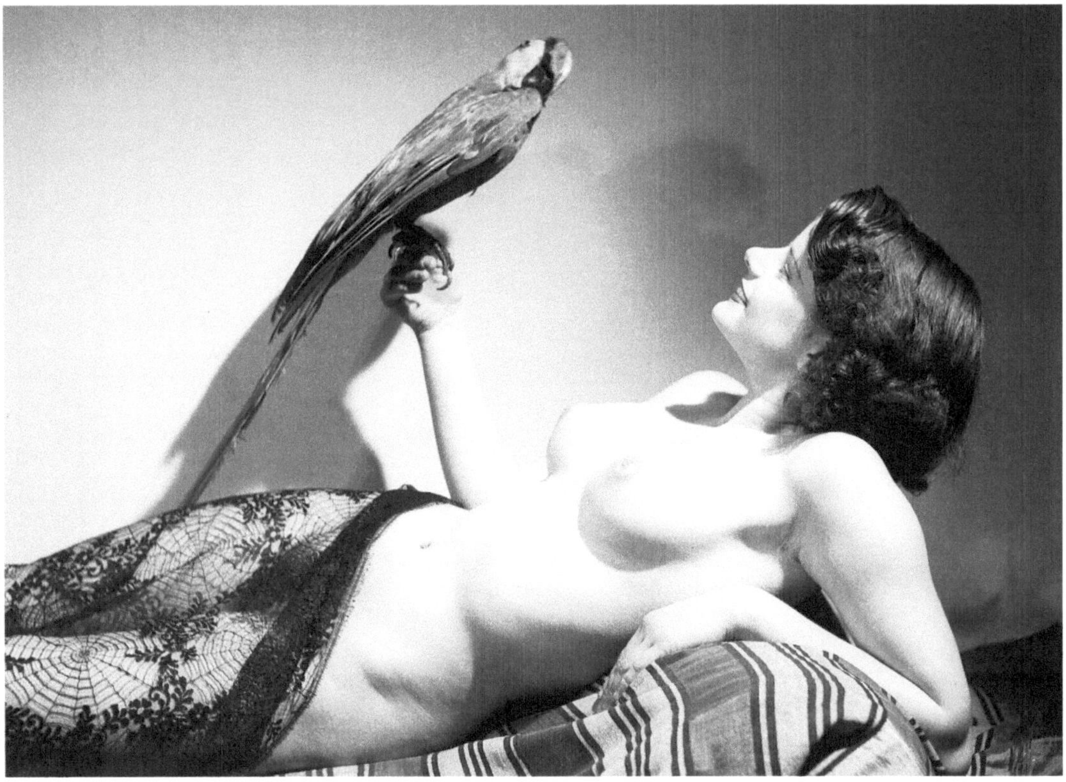

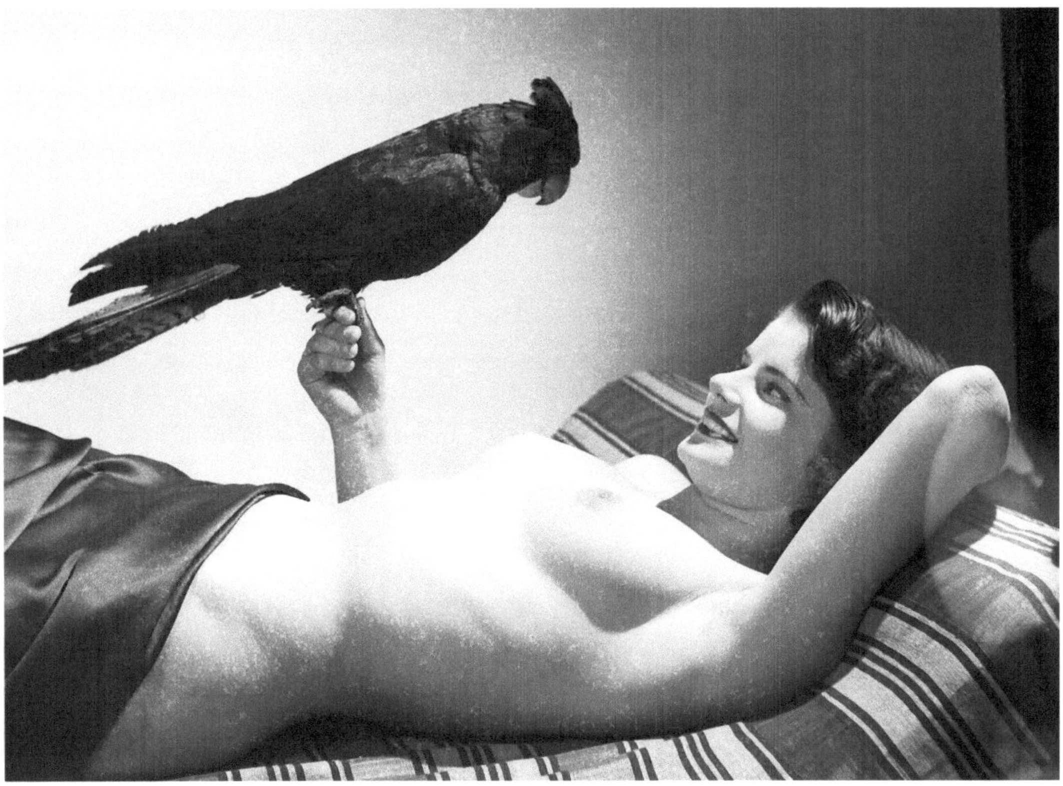

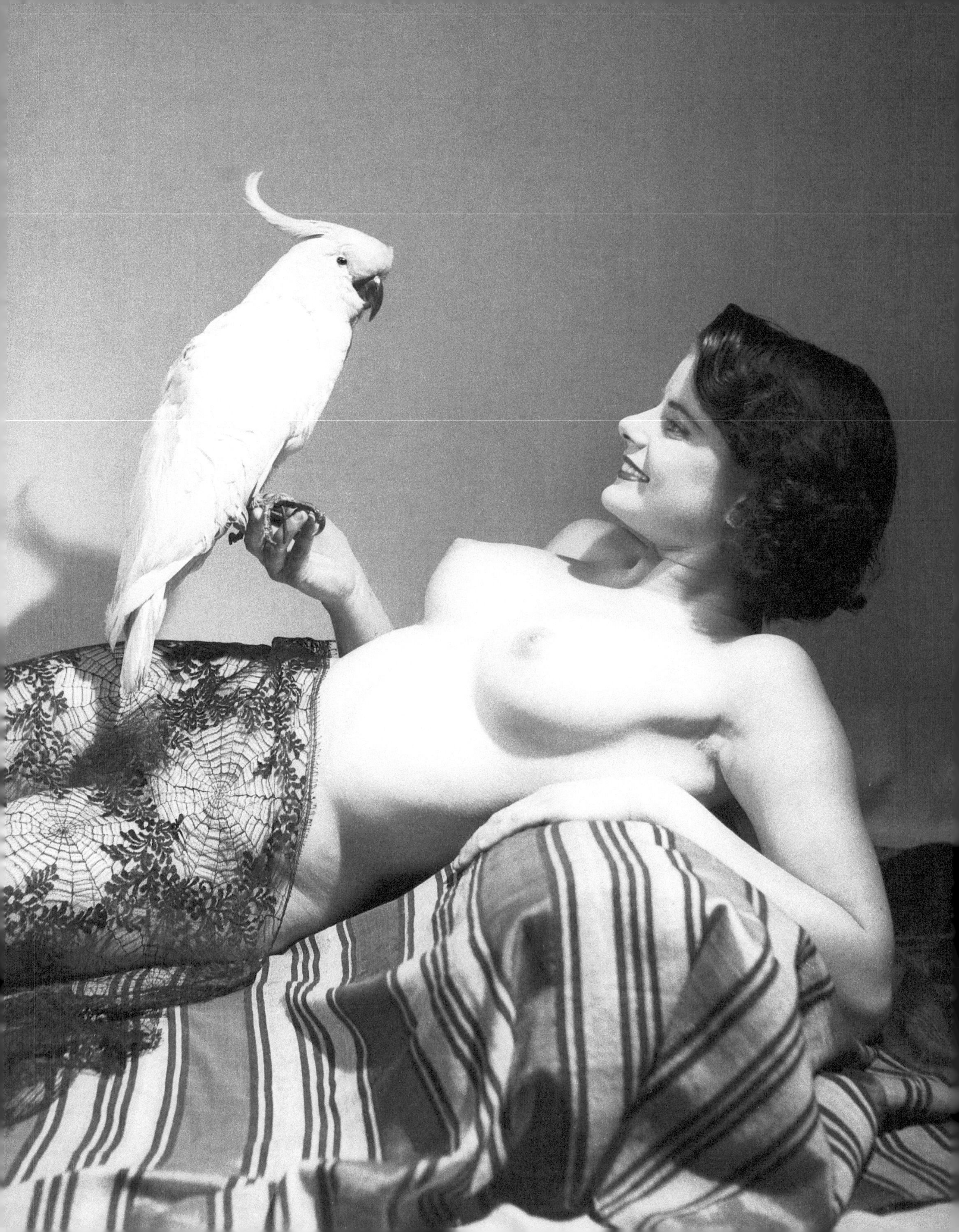

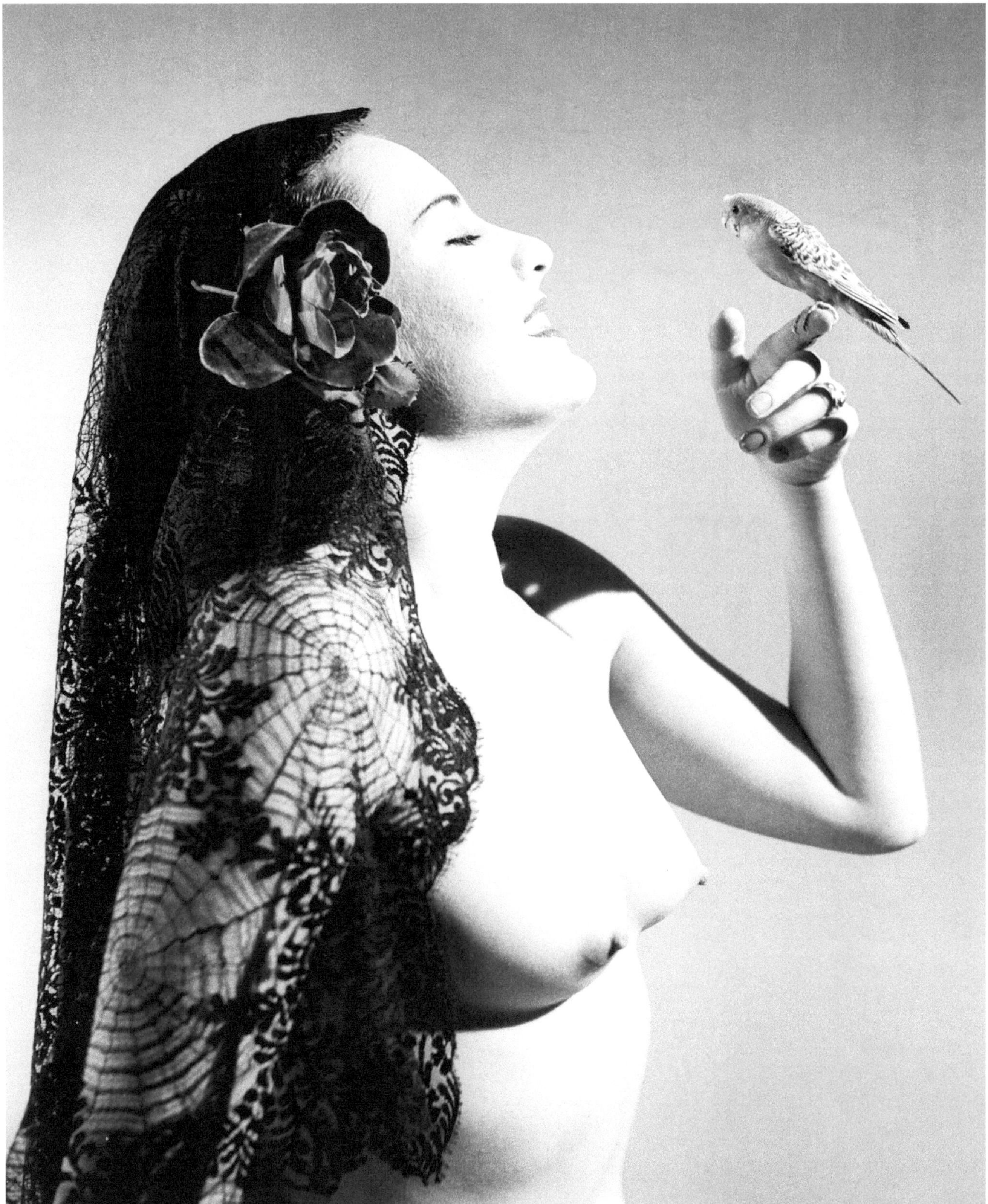

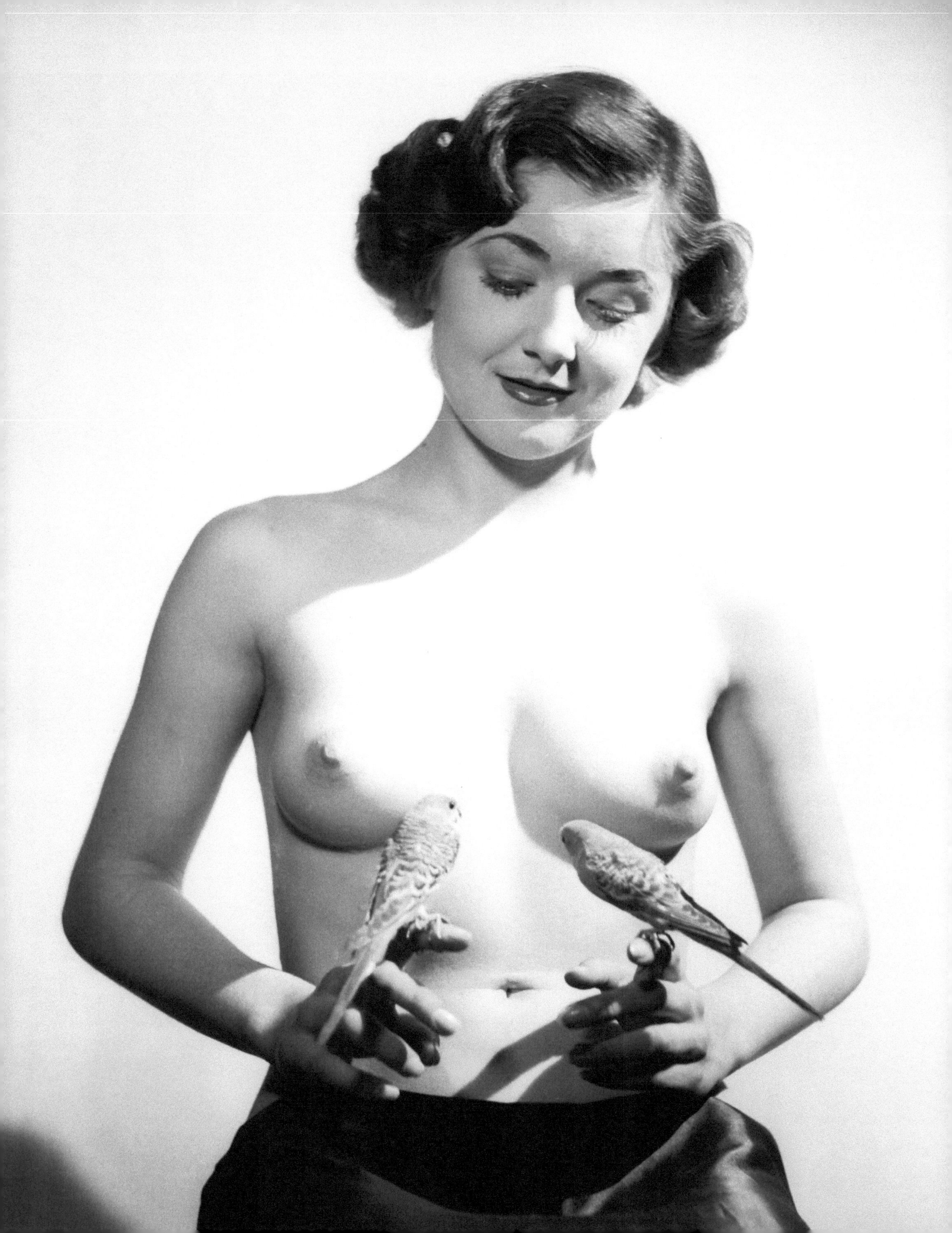

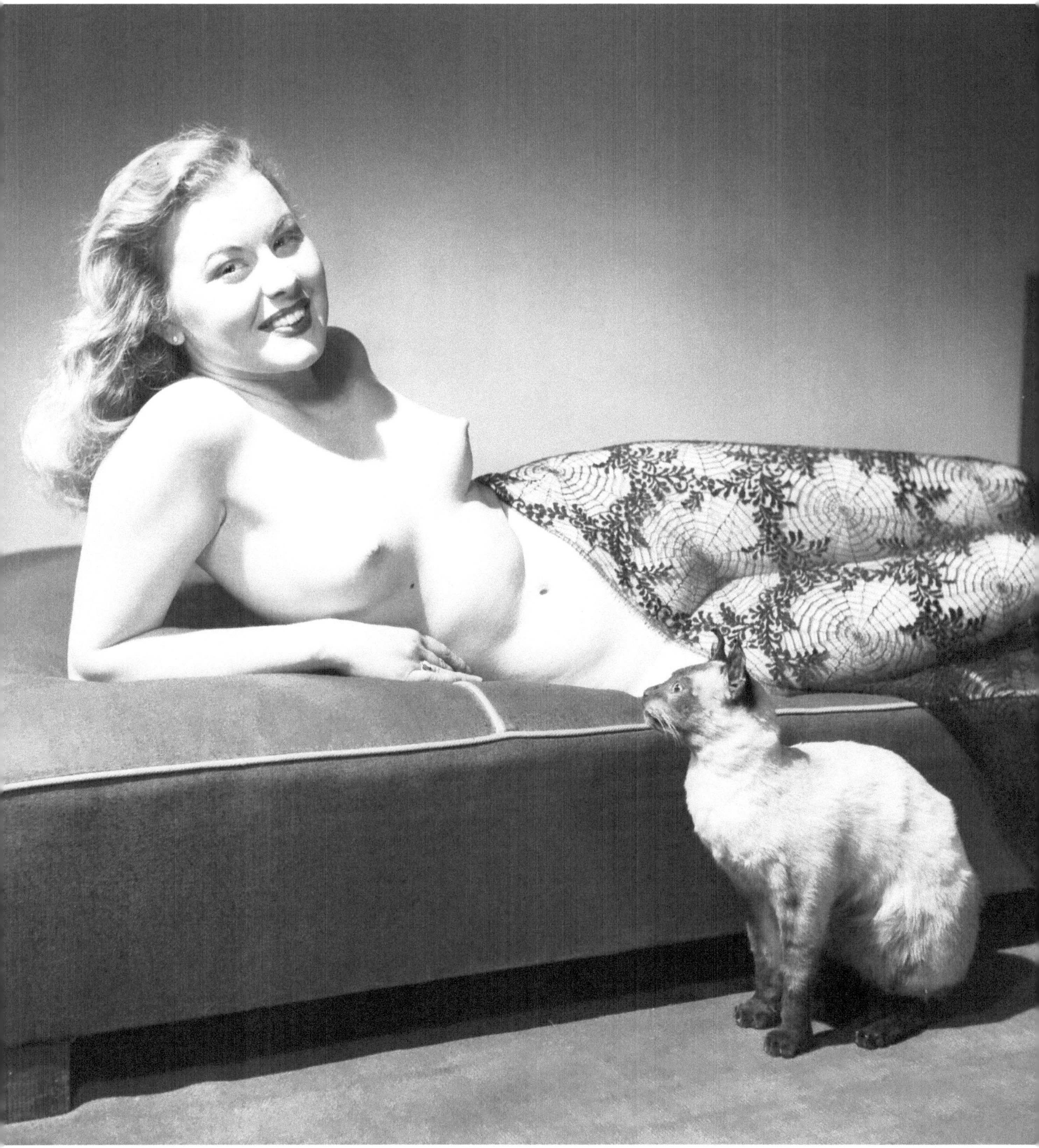

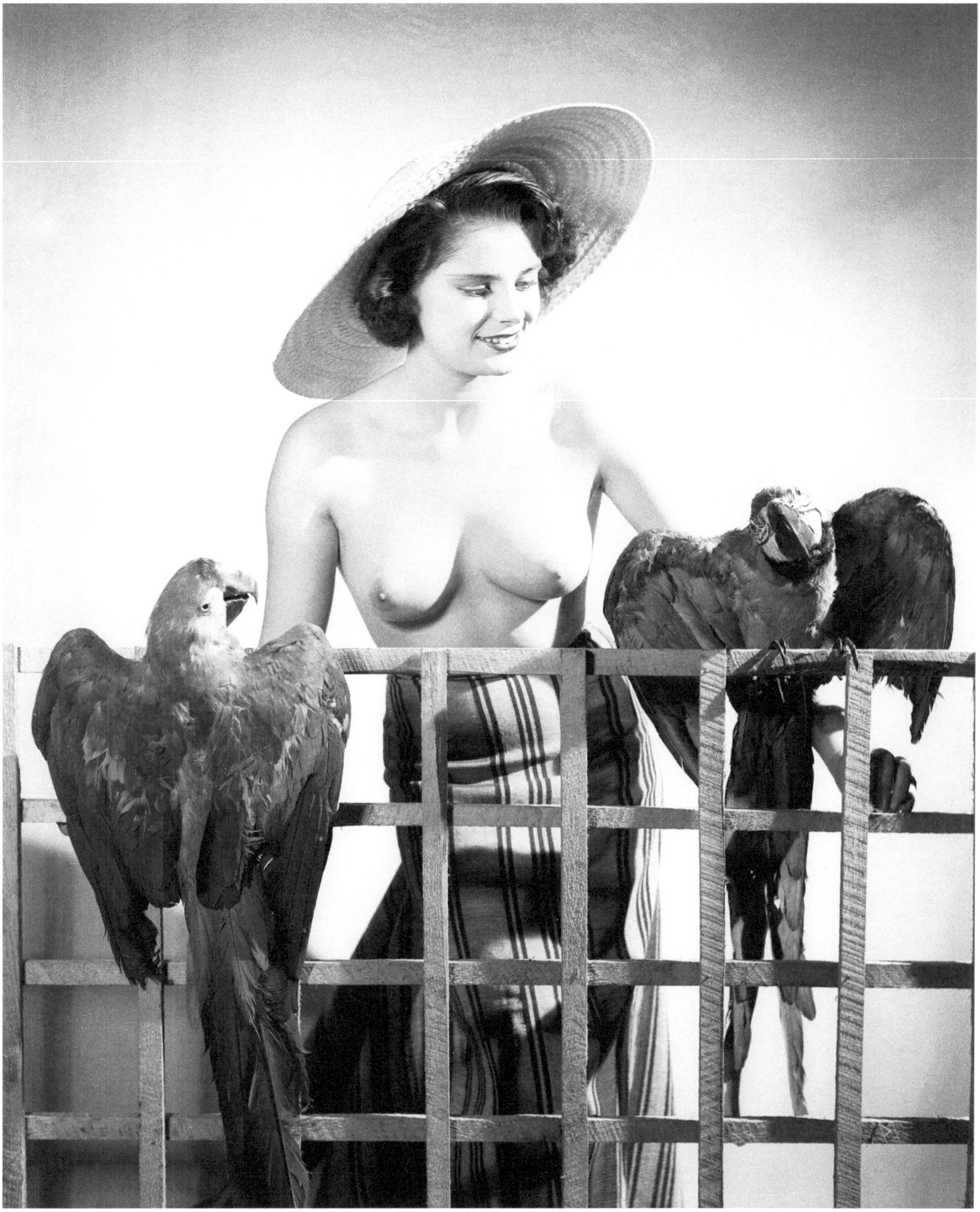

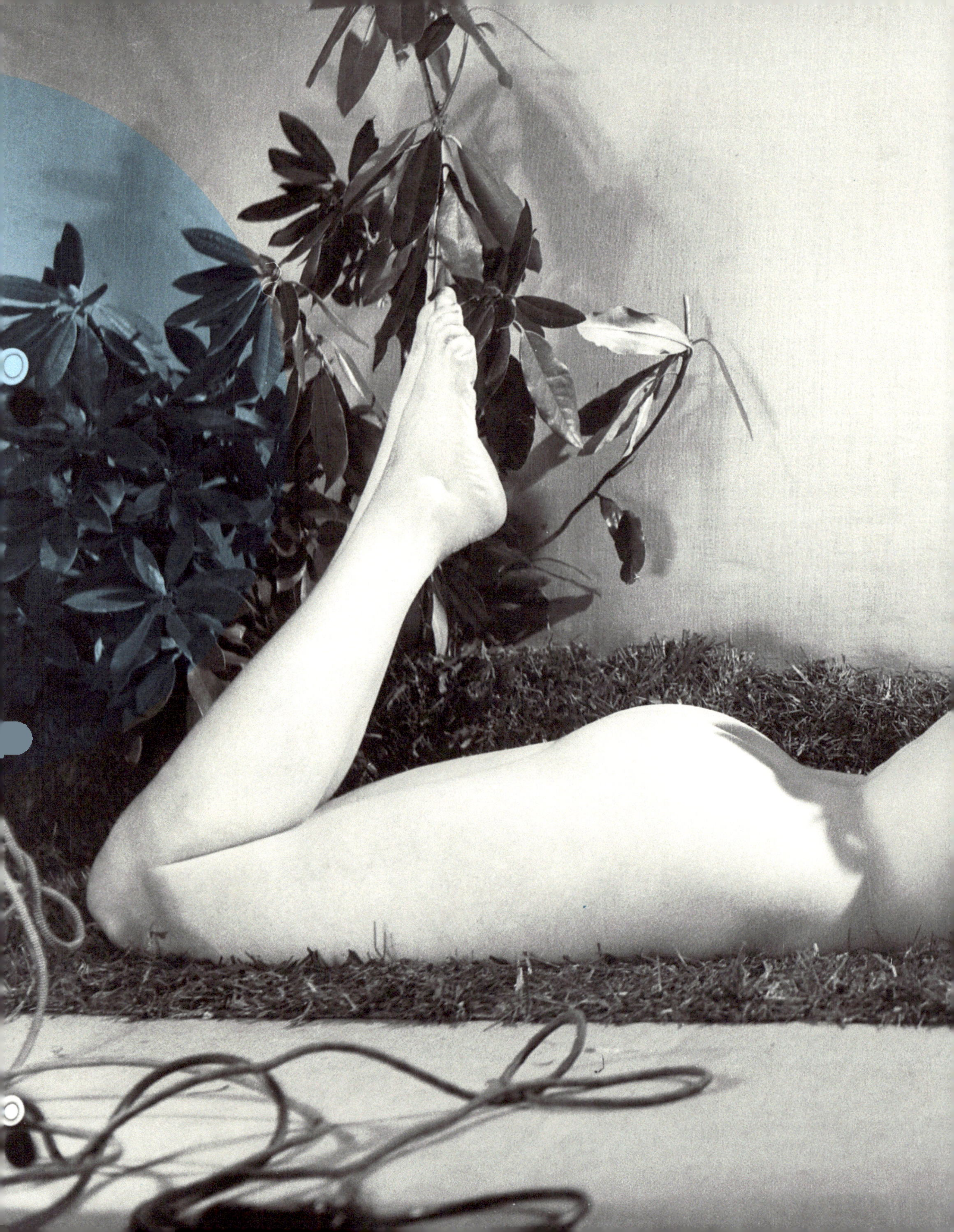

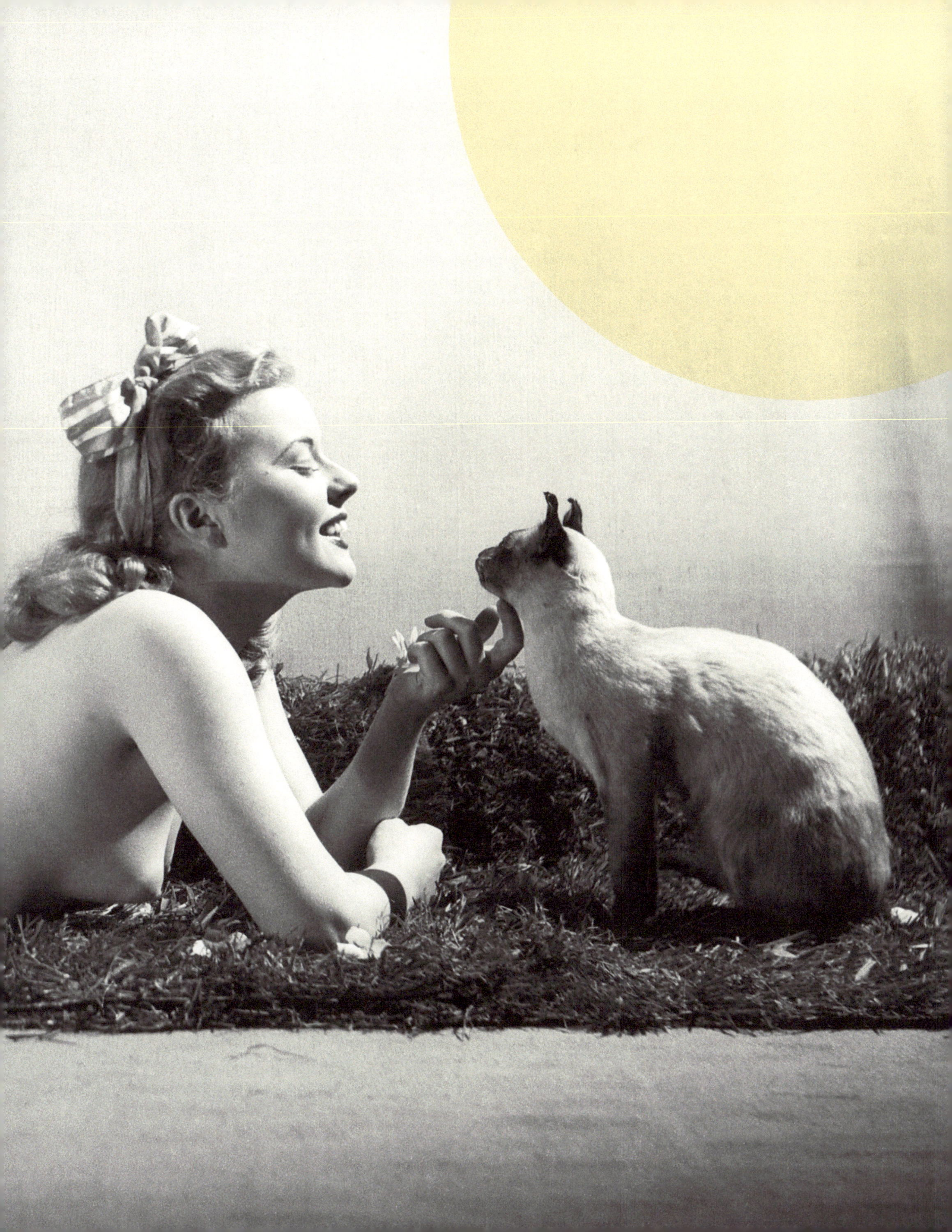

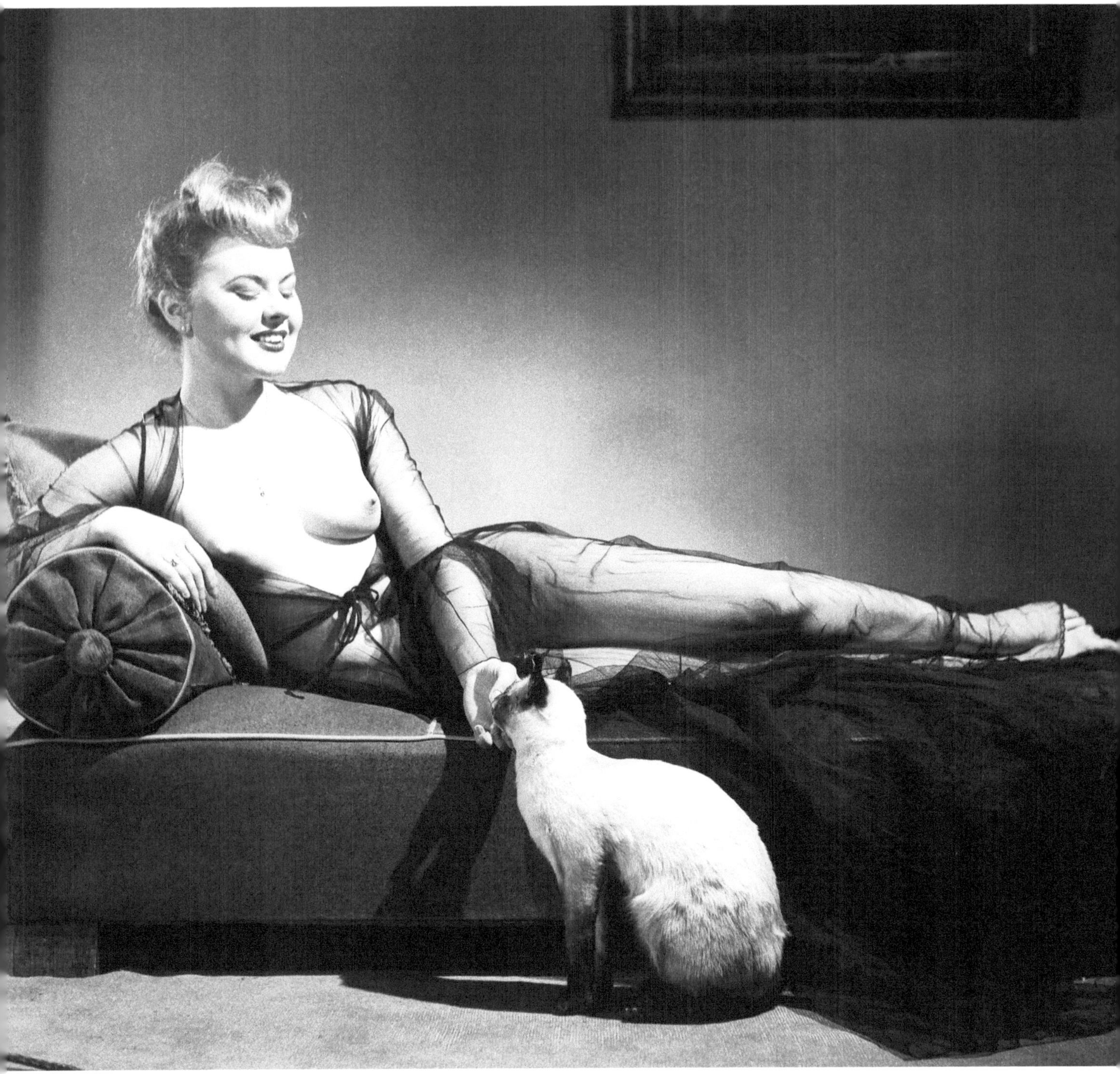

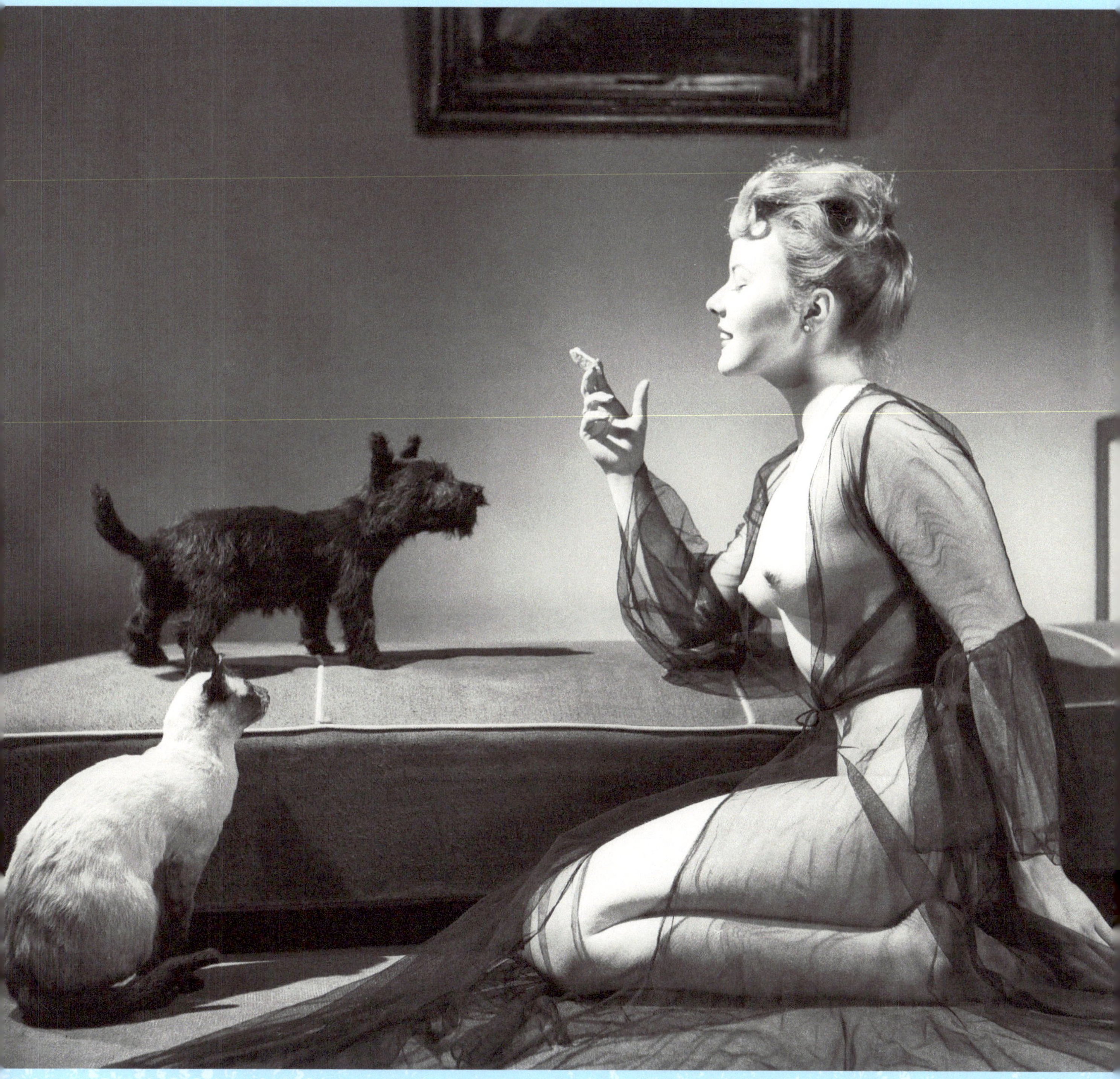

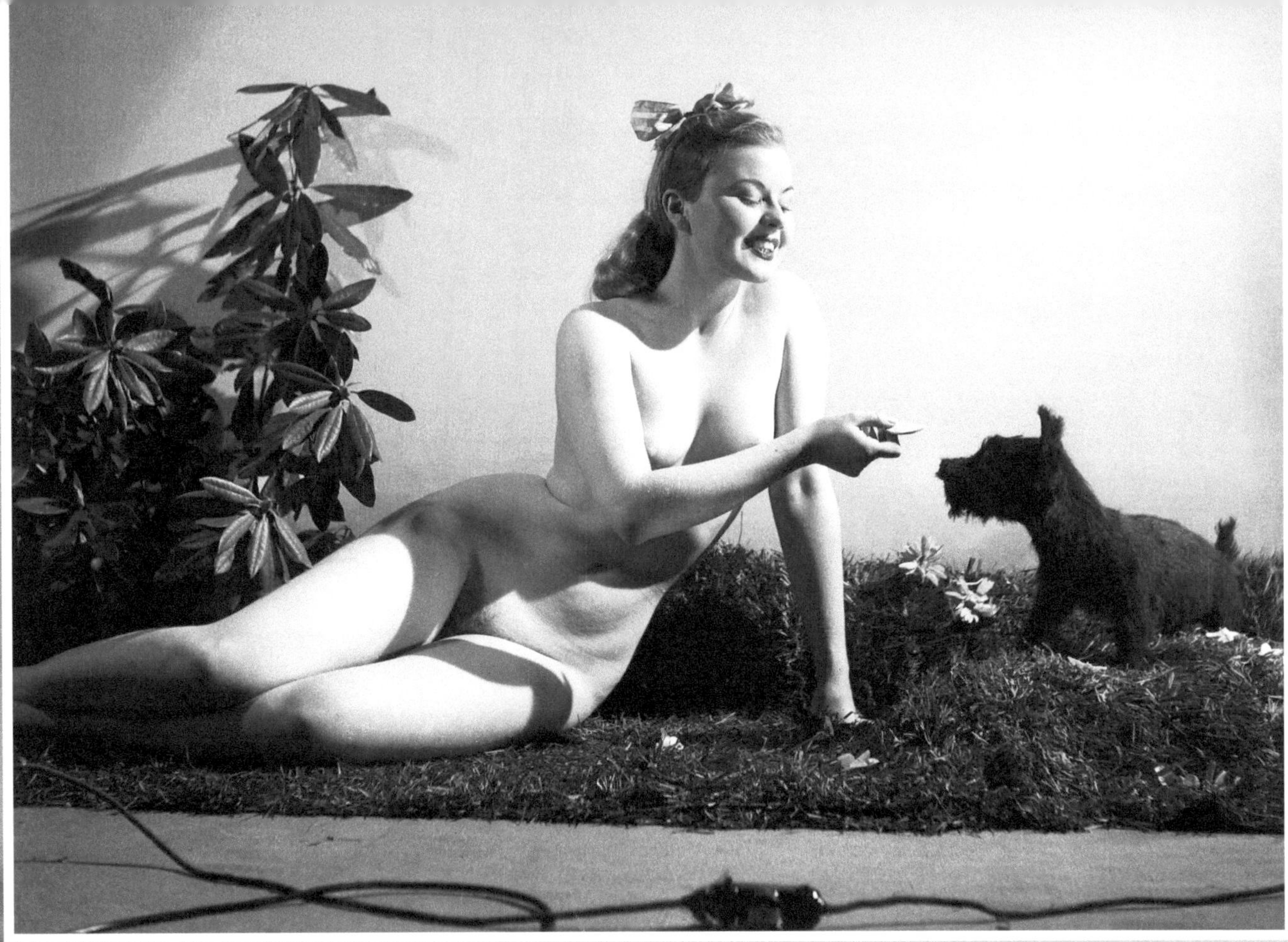

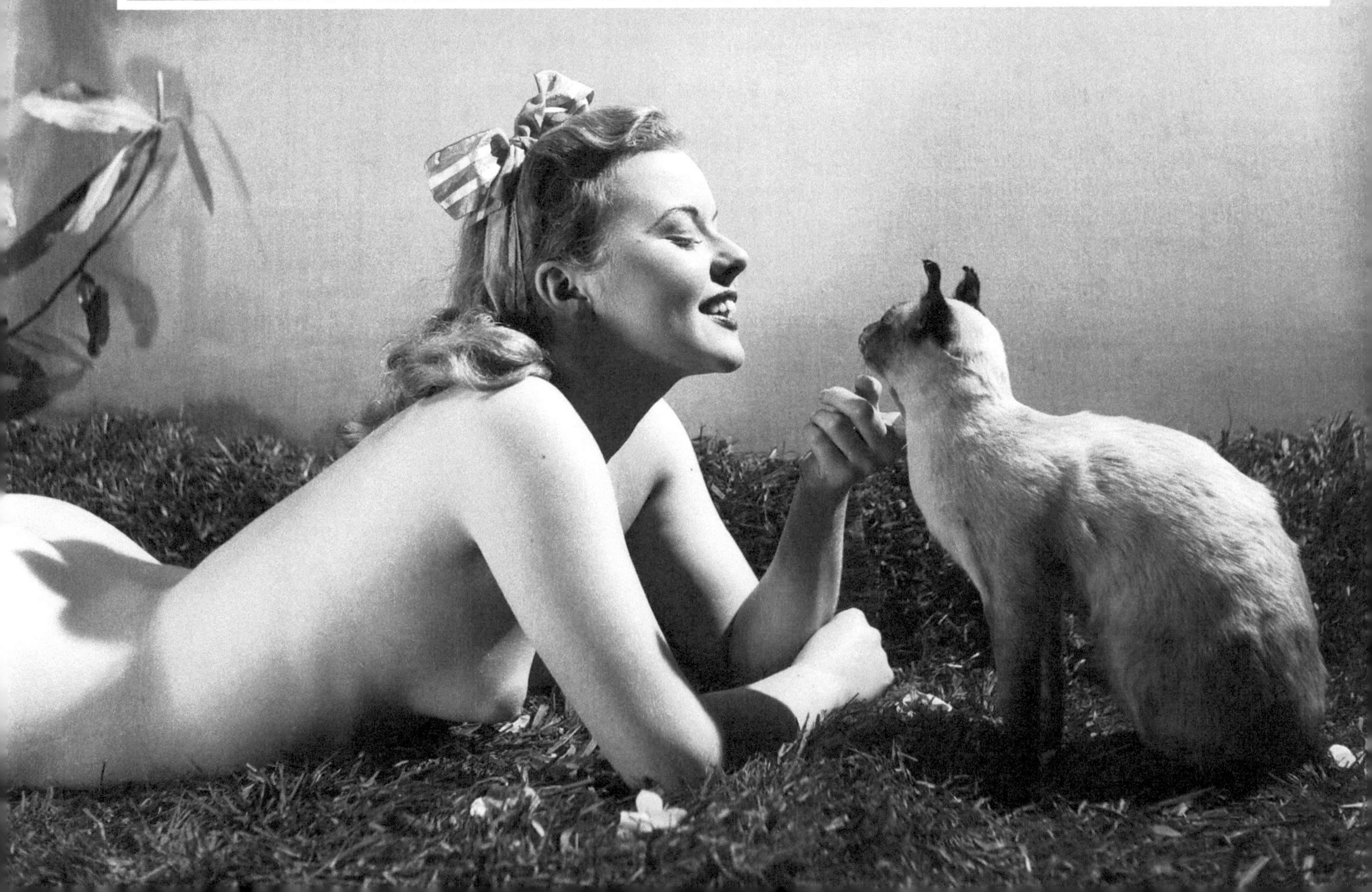

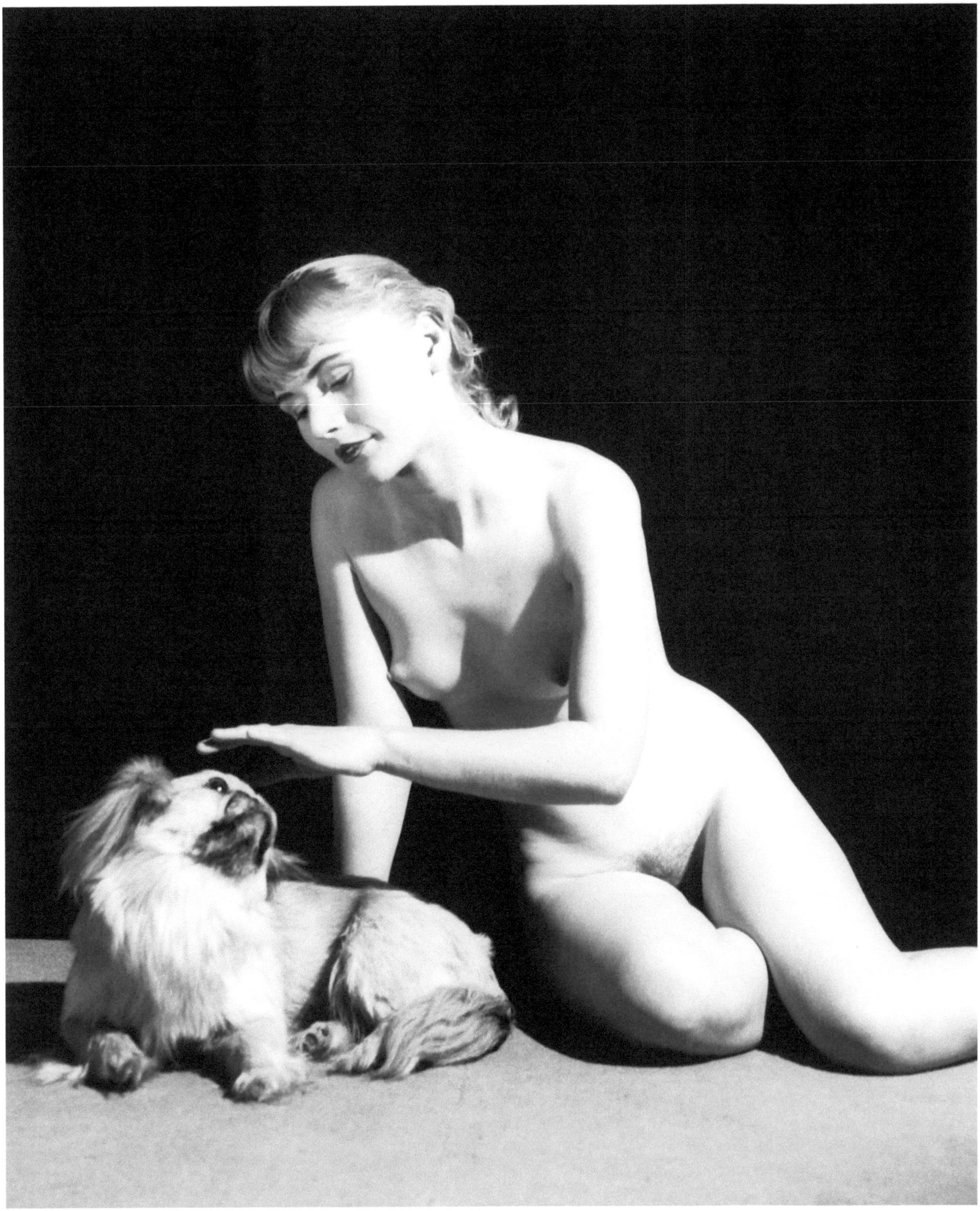

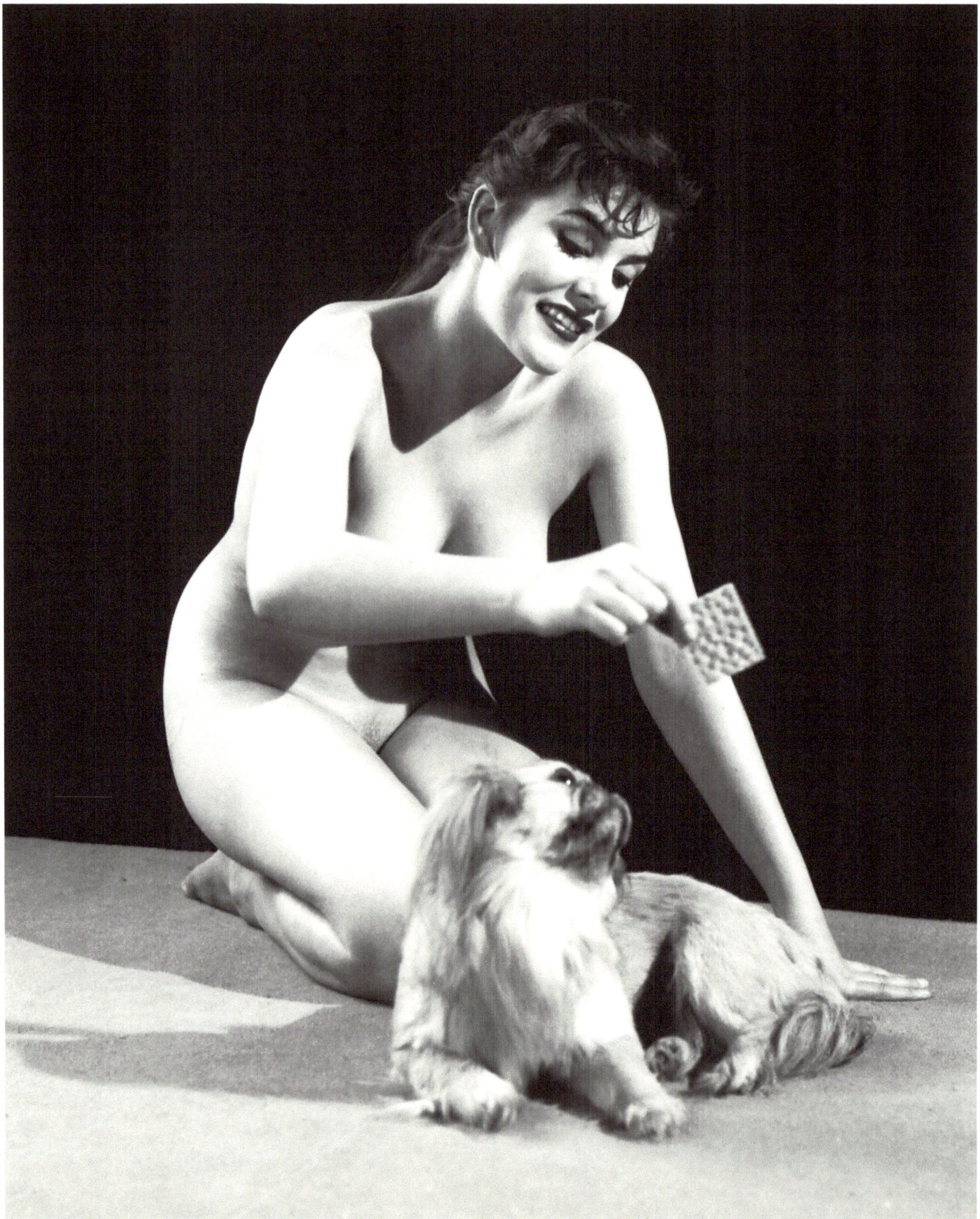

Above and right: June Wilkinson.

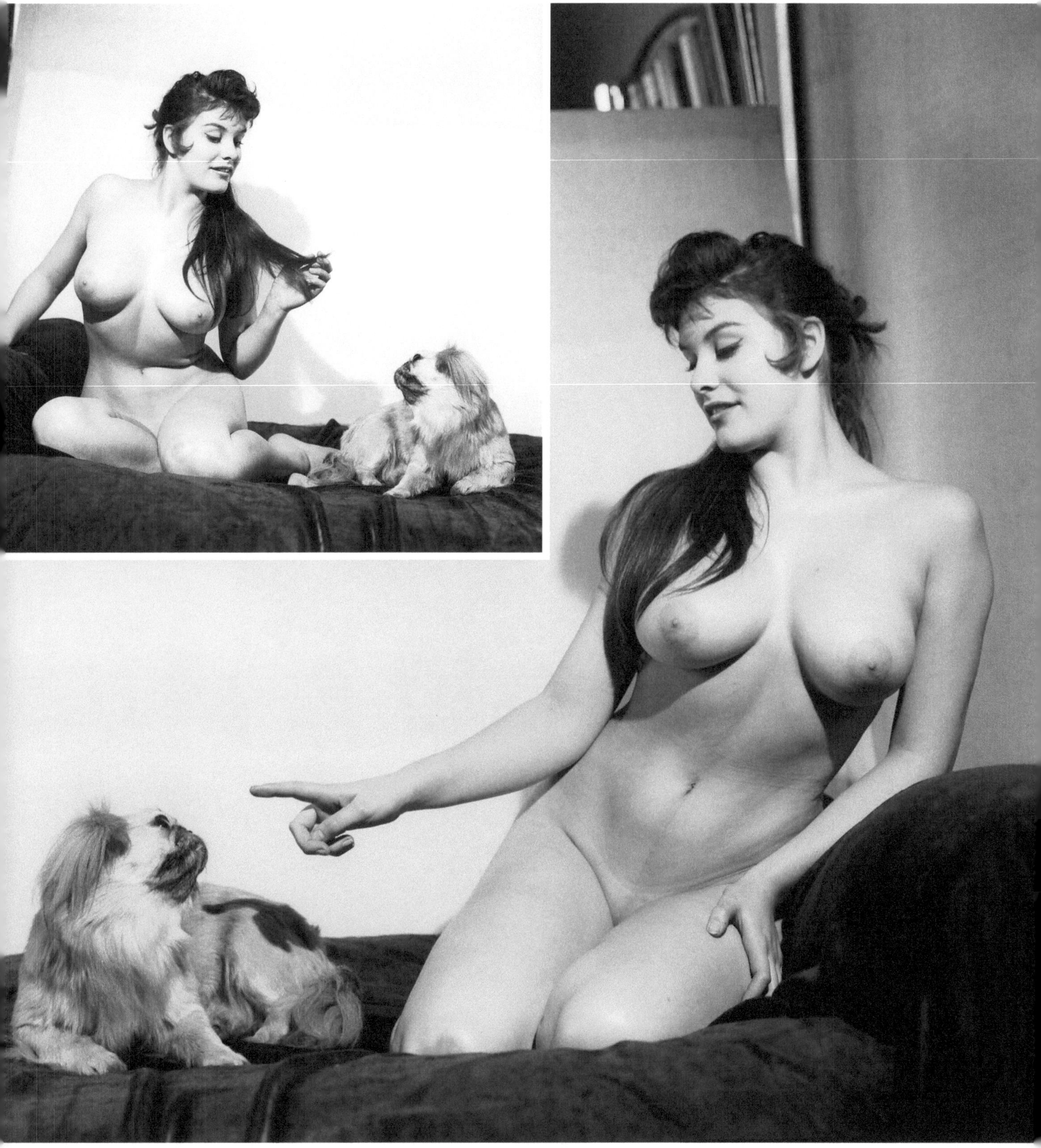

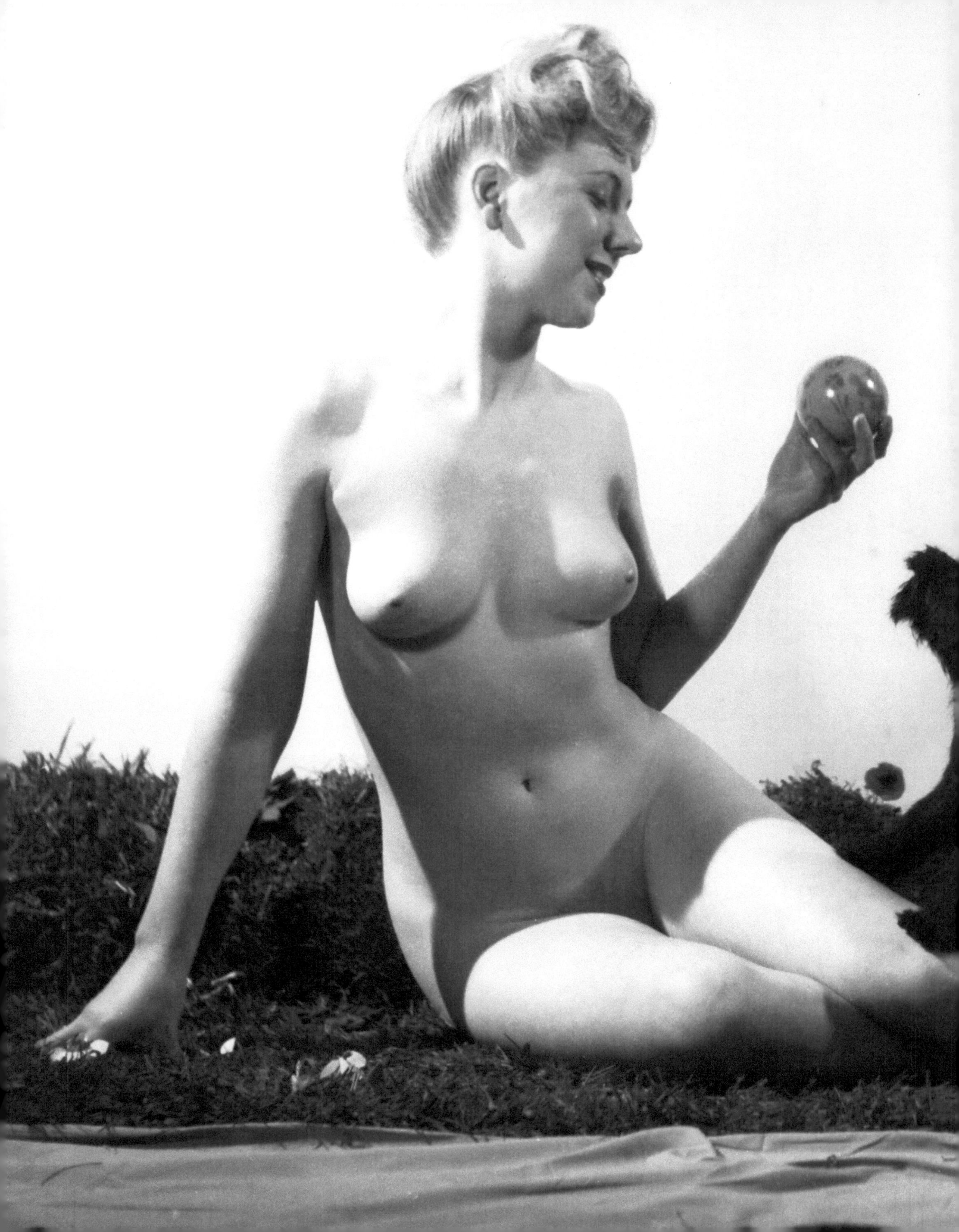

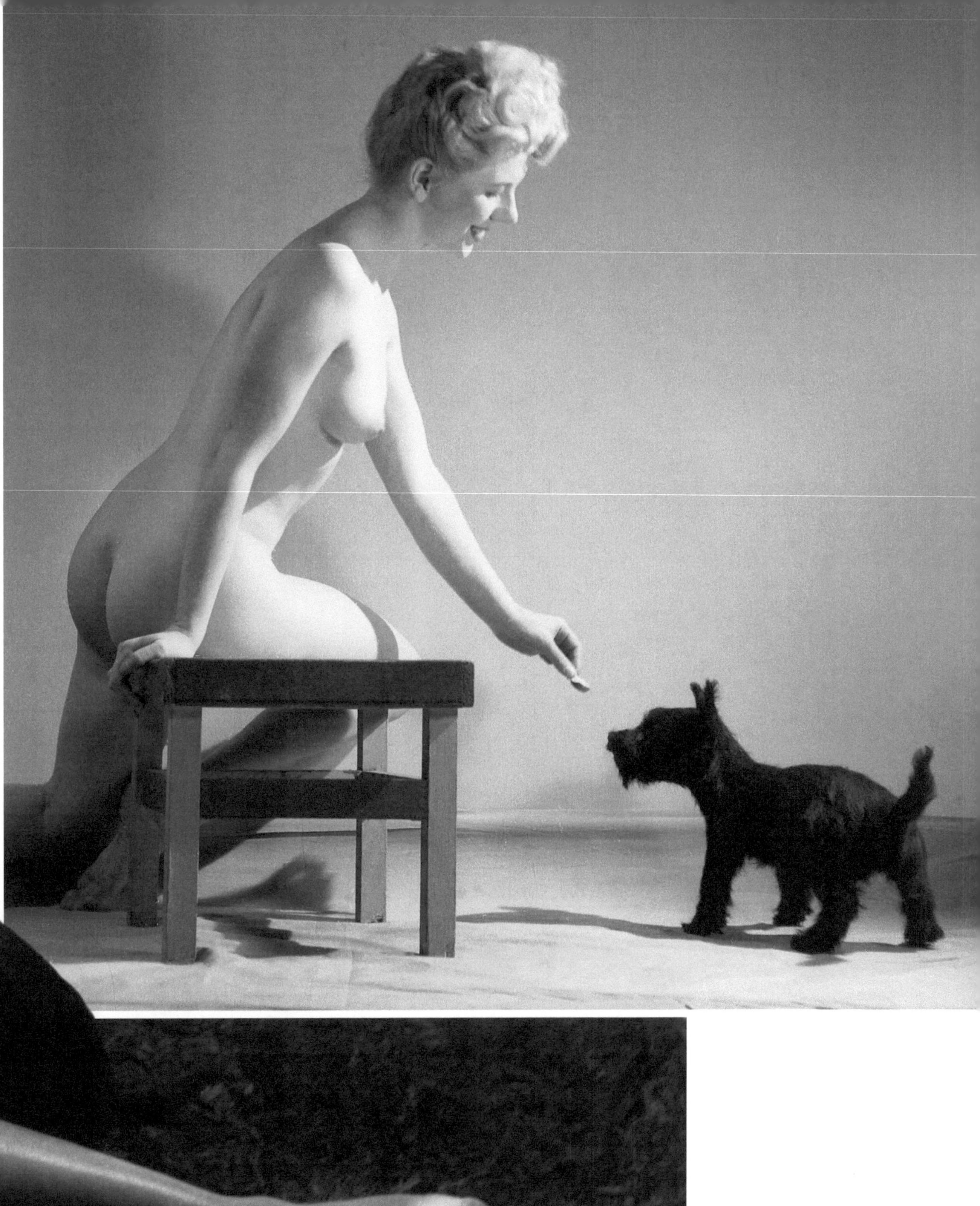

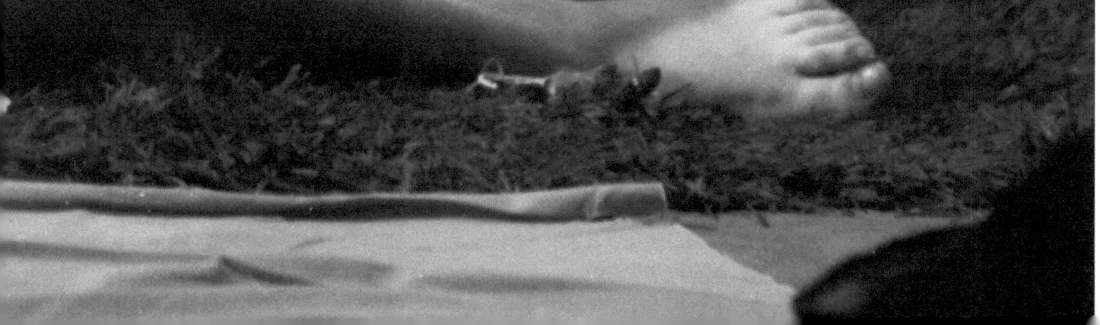

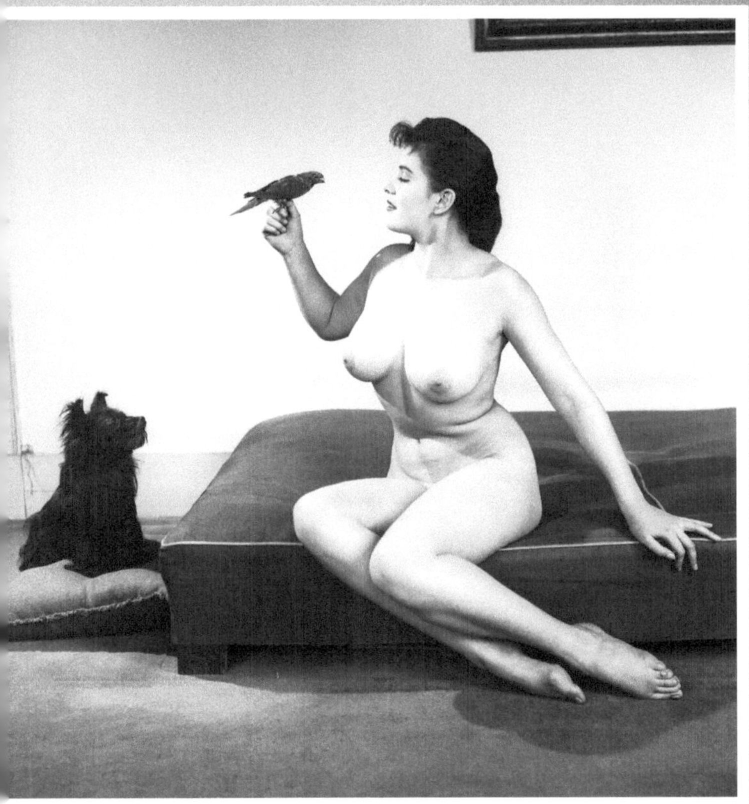

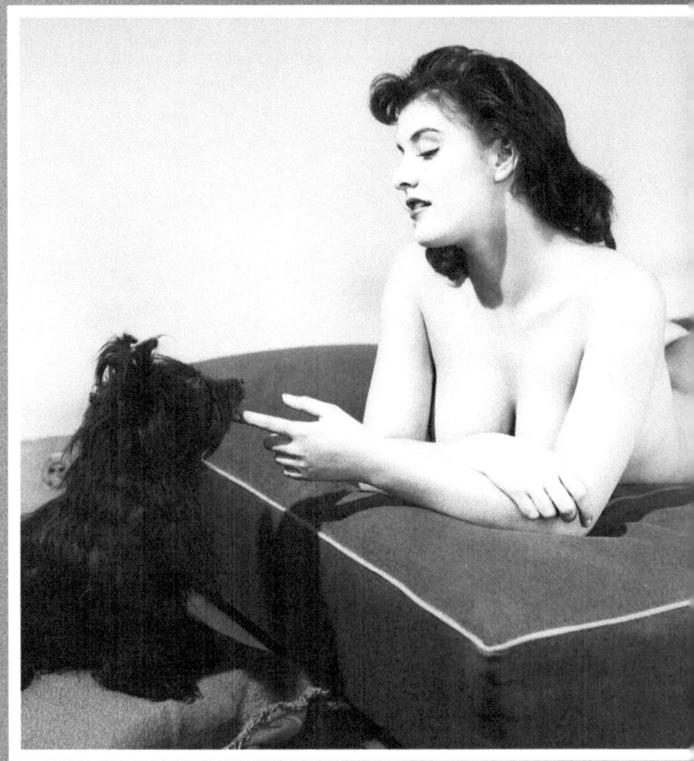

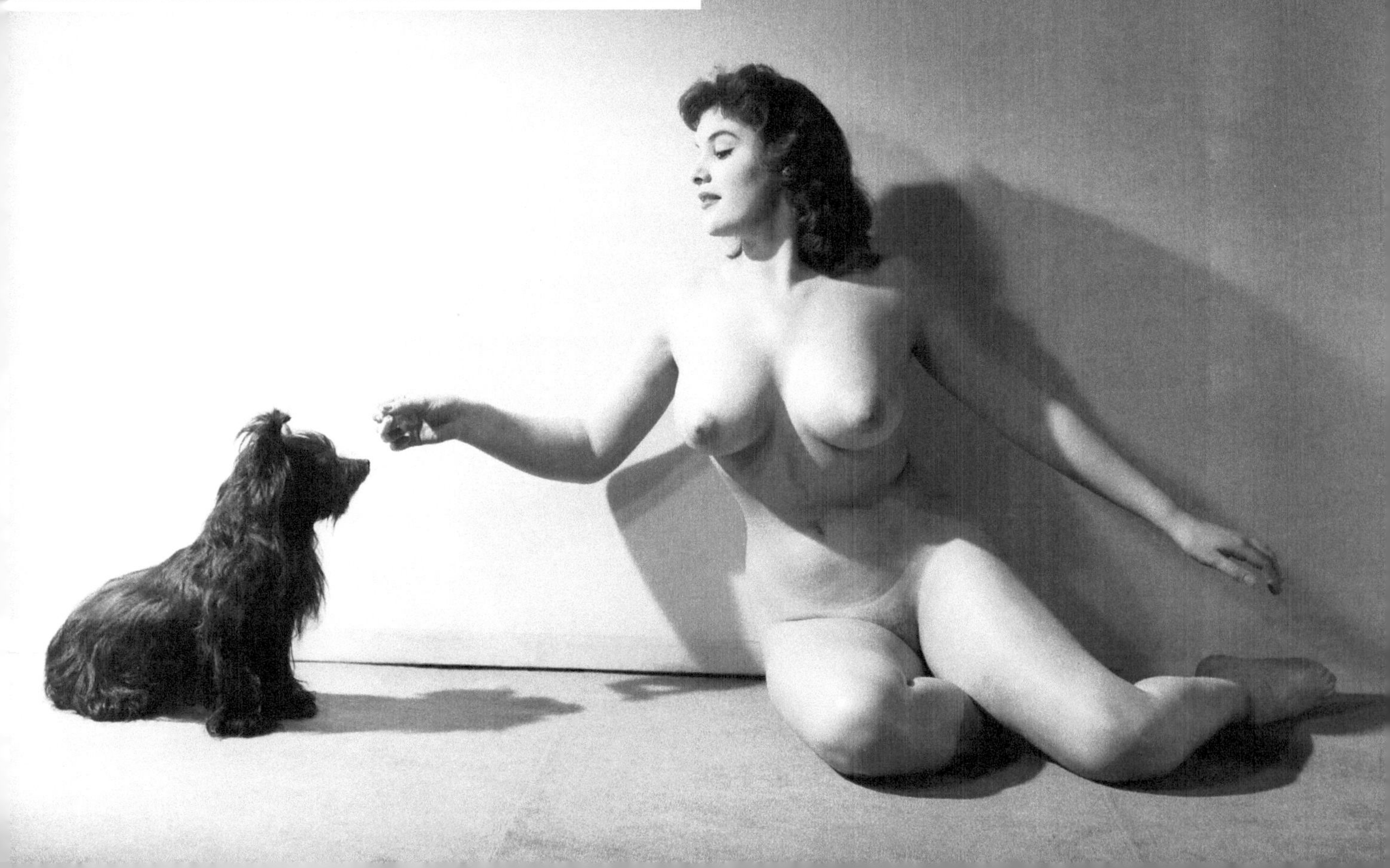

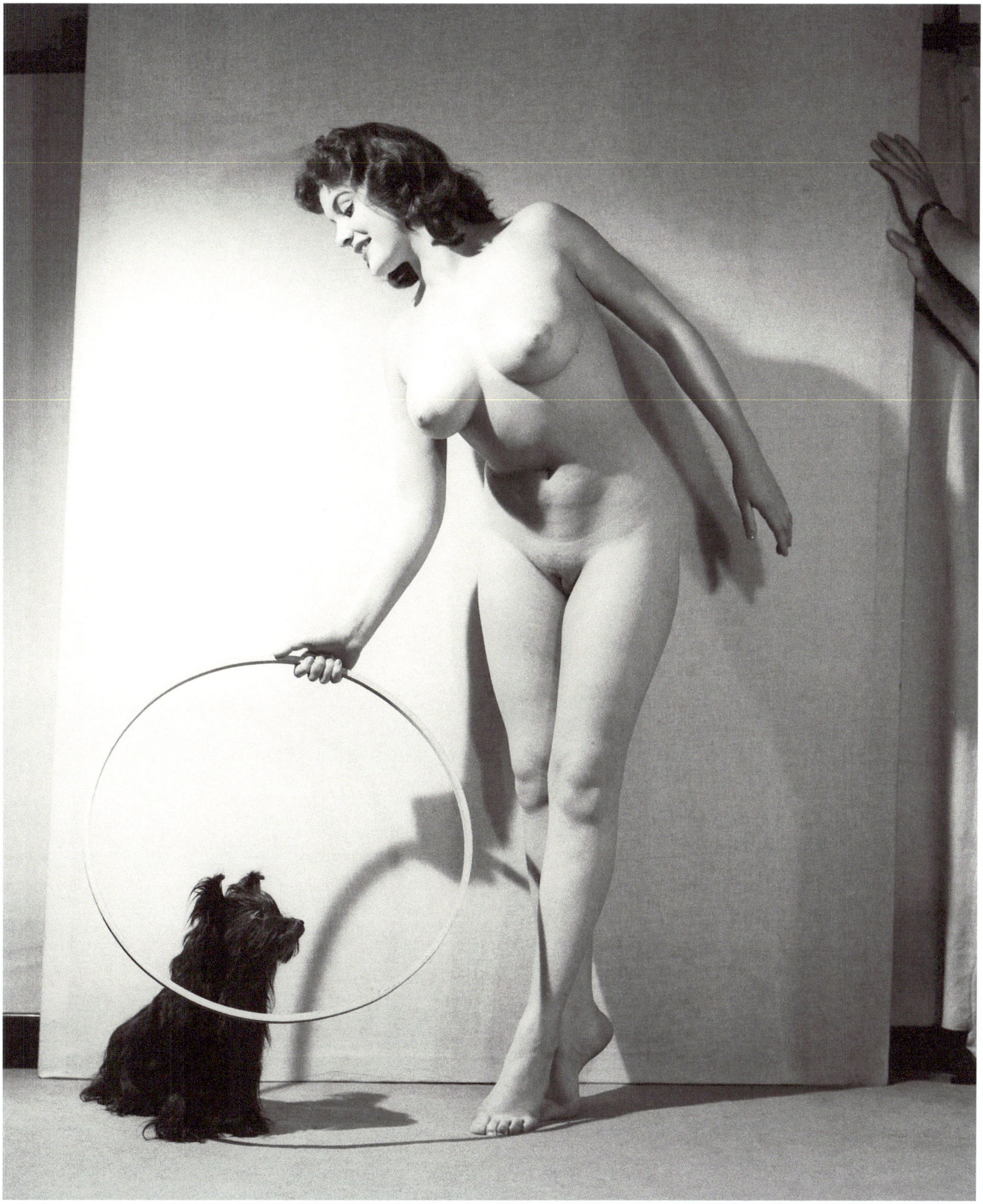

Left and above: June Wilkinson who at the age of 15 was the youngest topless performer at the Windmill Theatre in London.

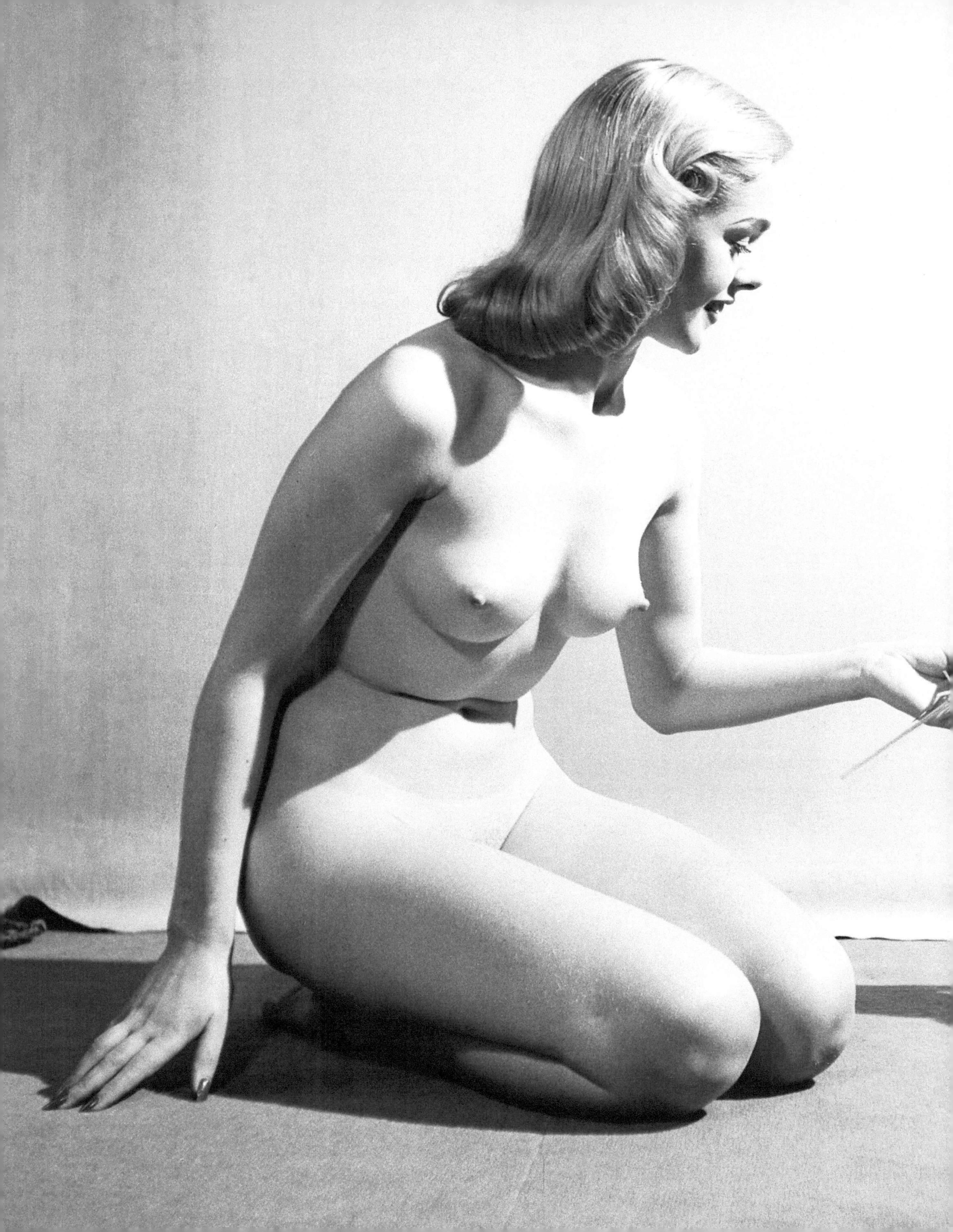

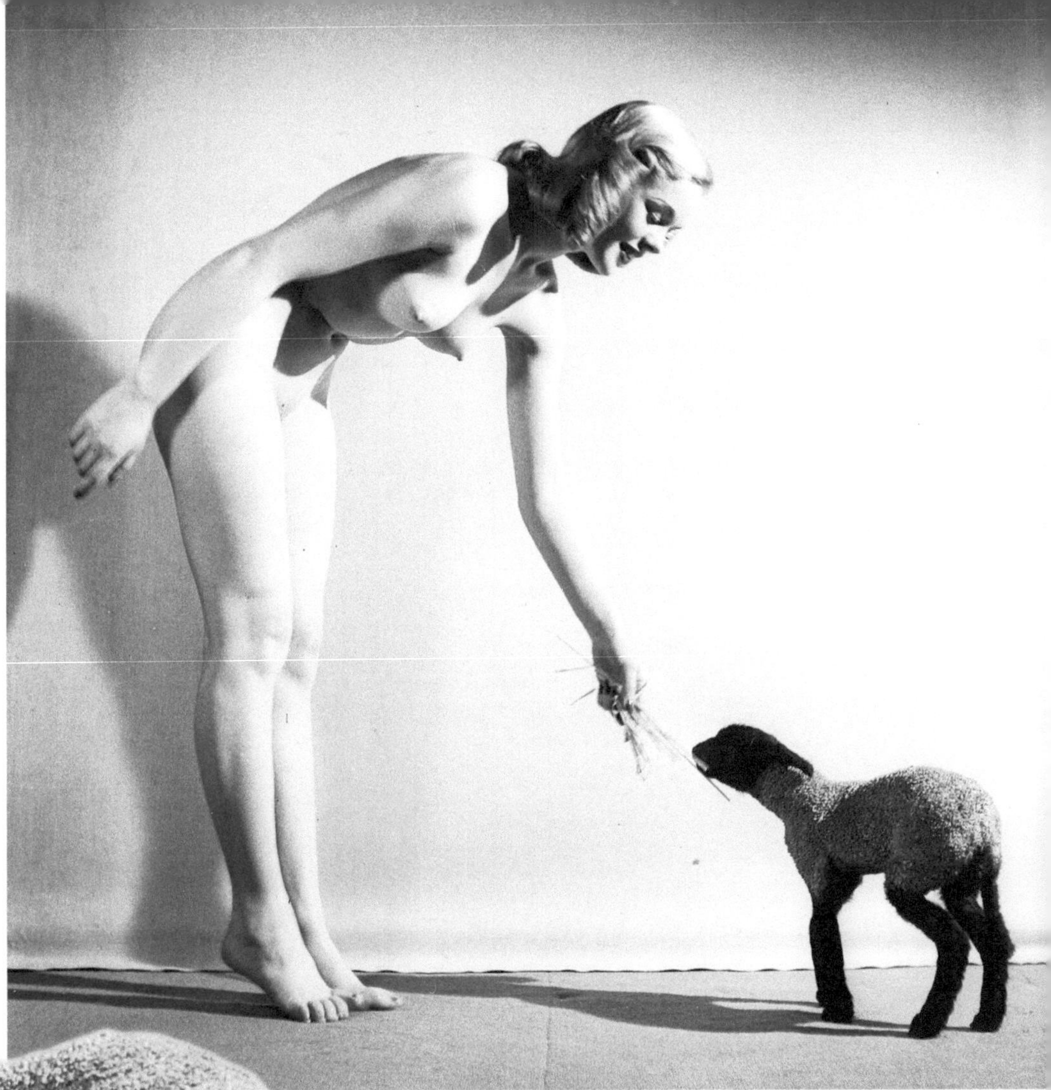

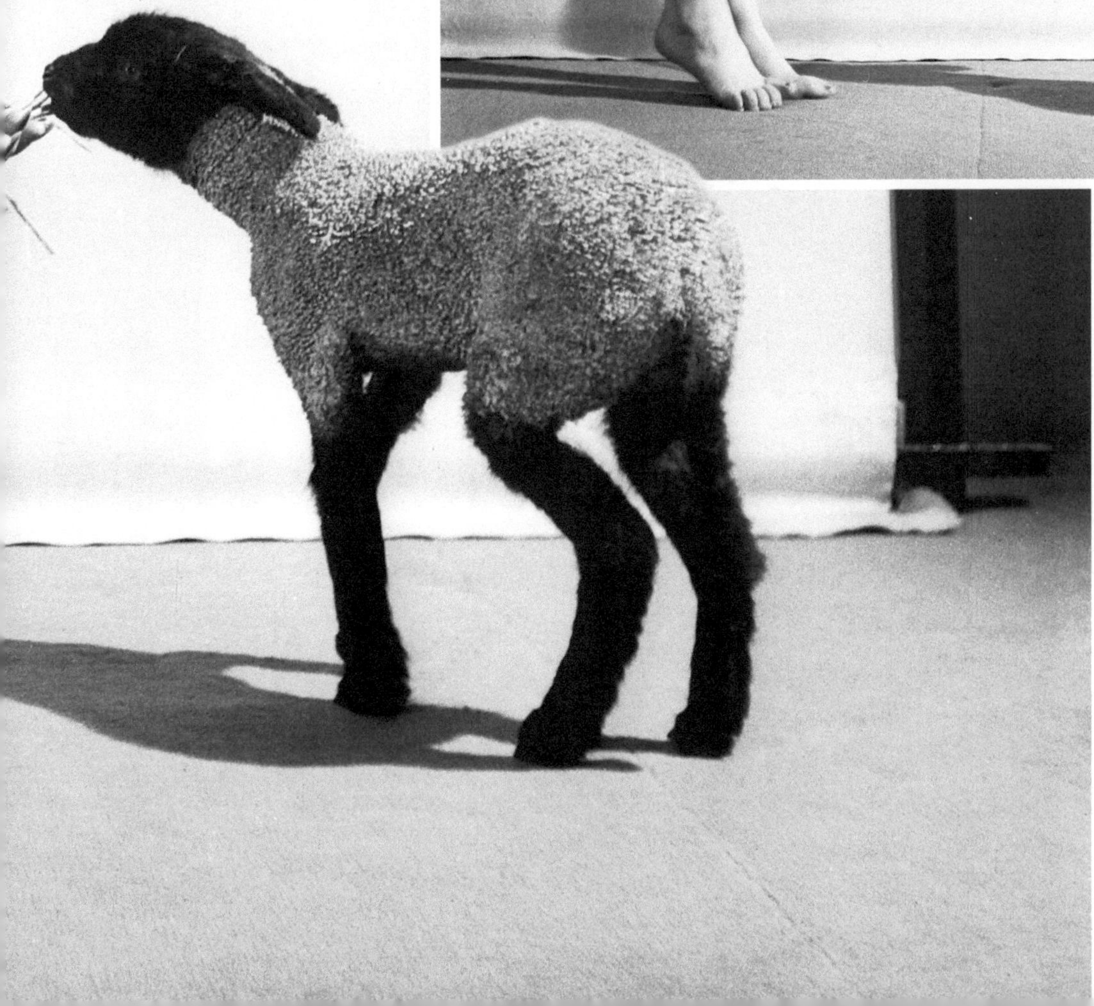

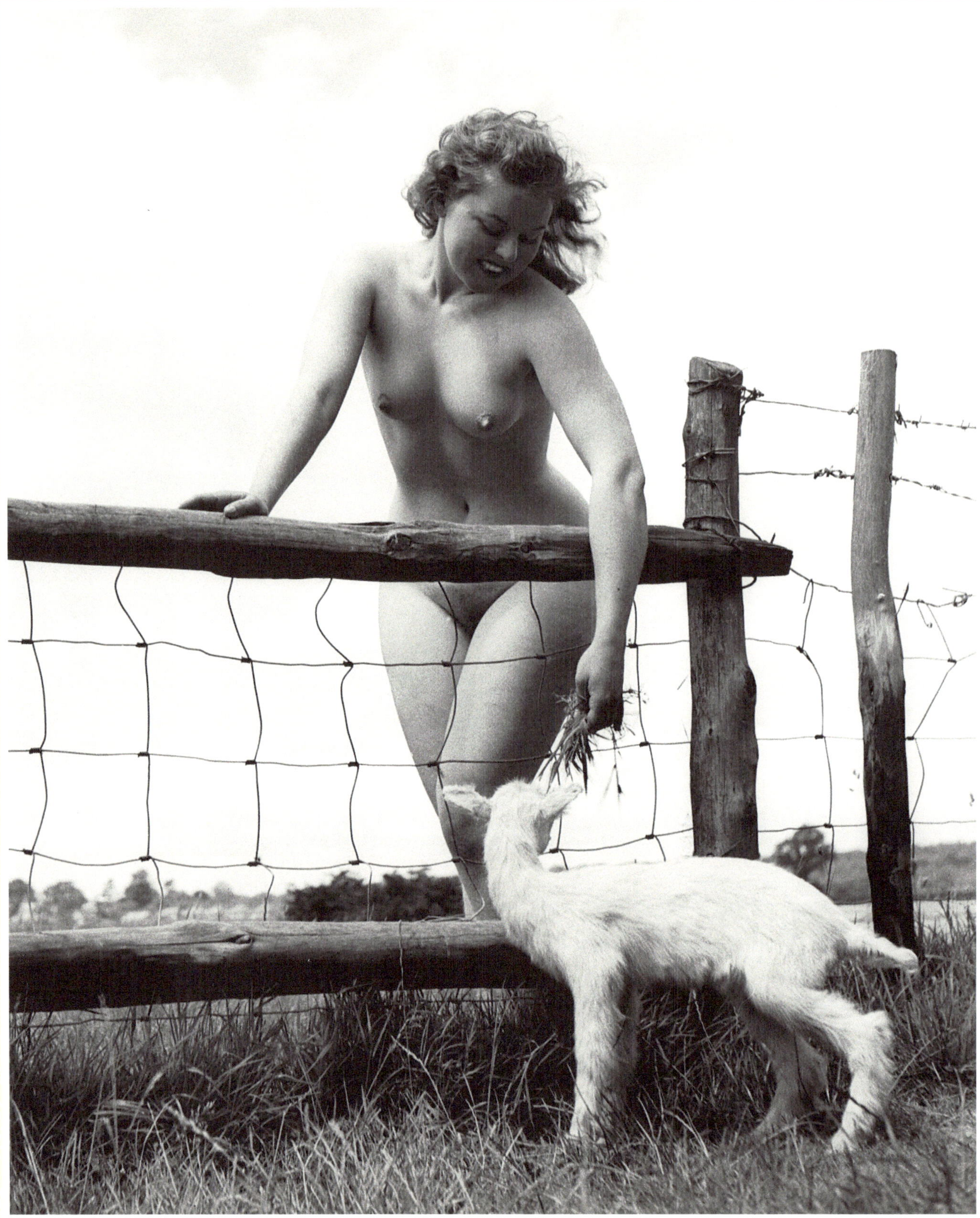

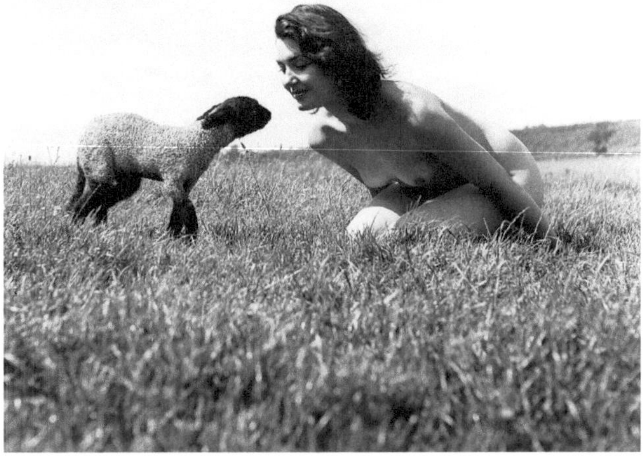

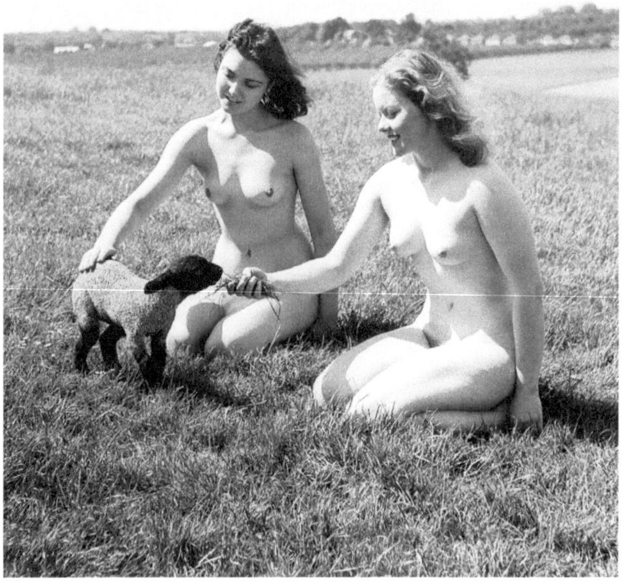

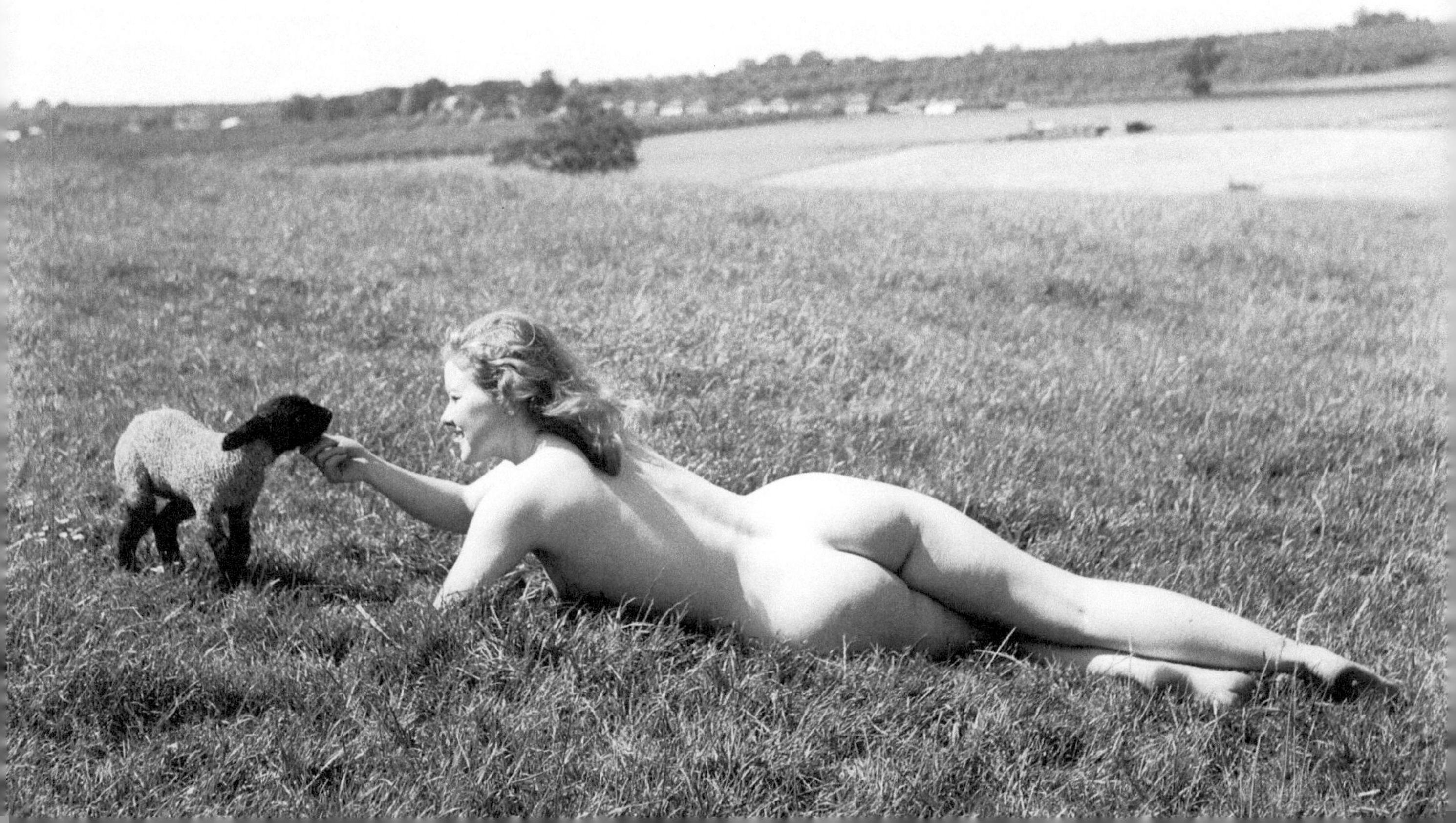

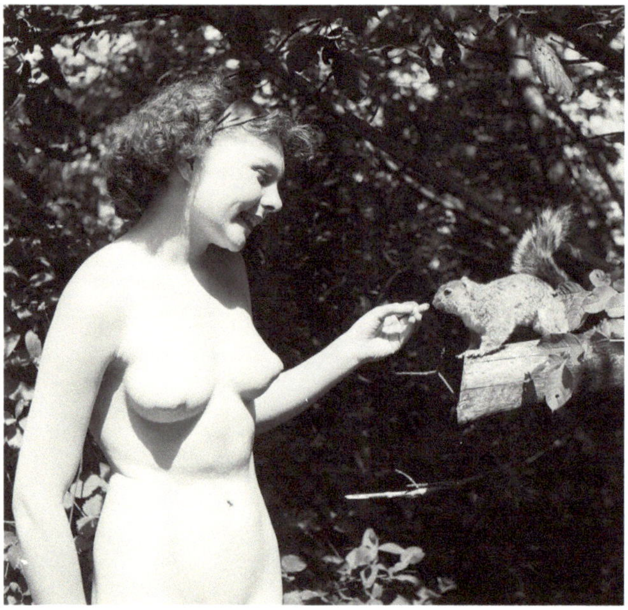

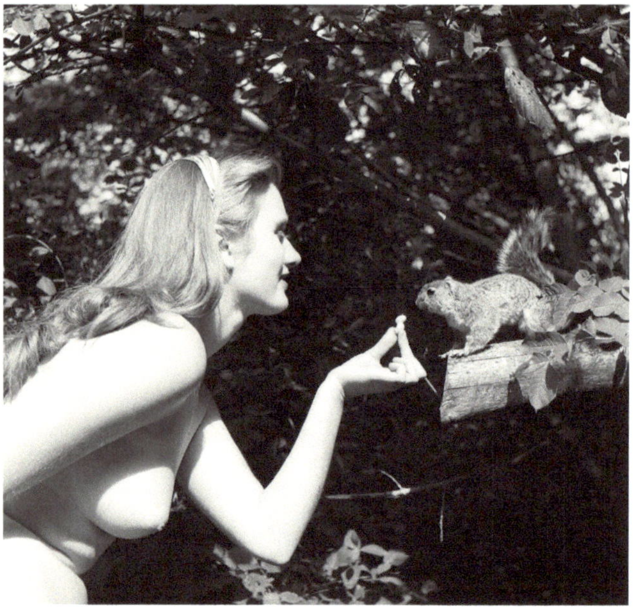

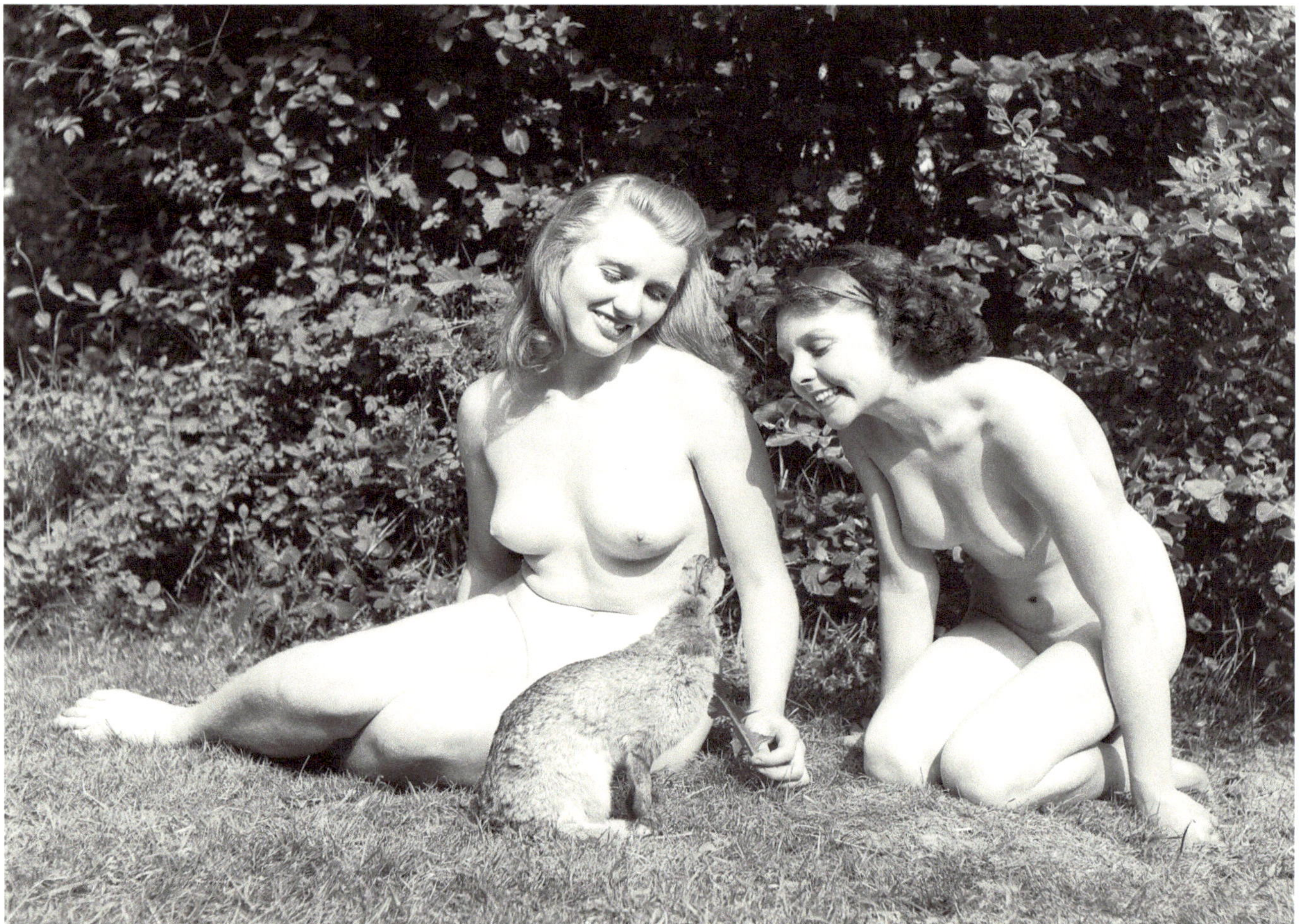

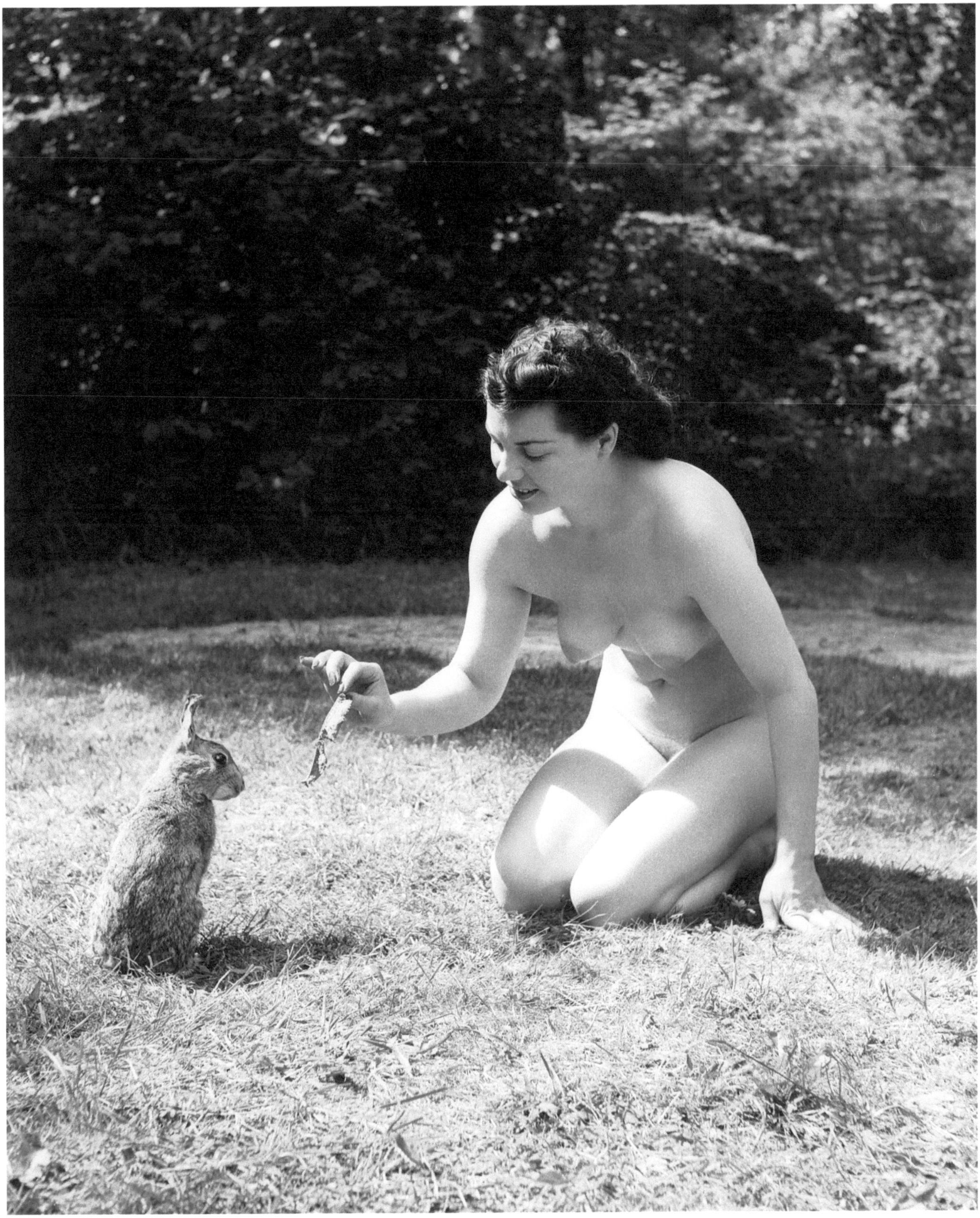

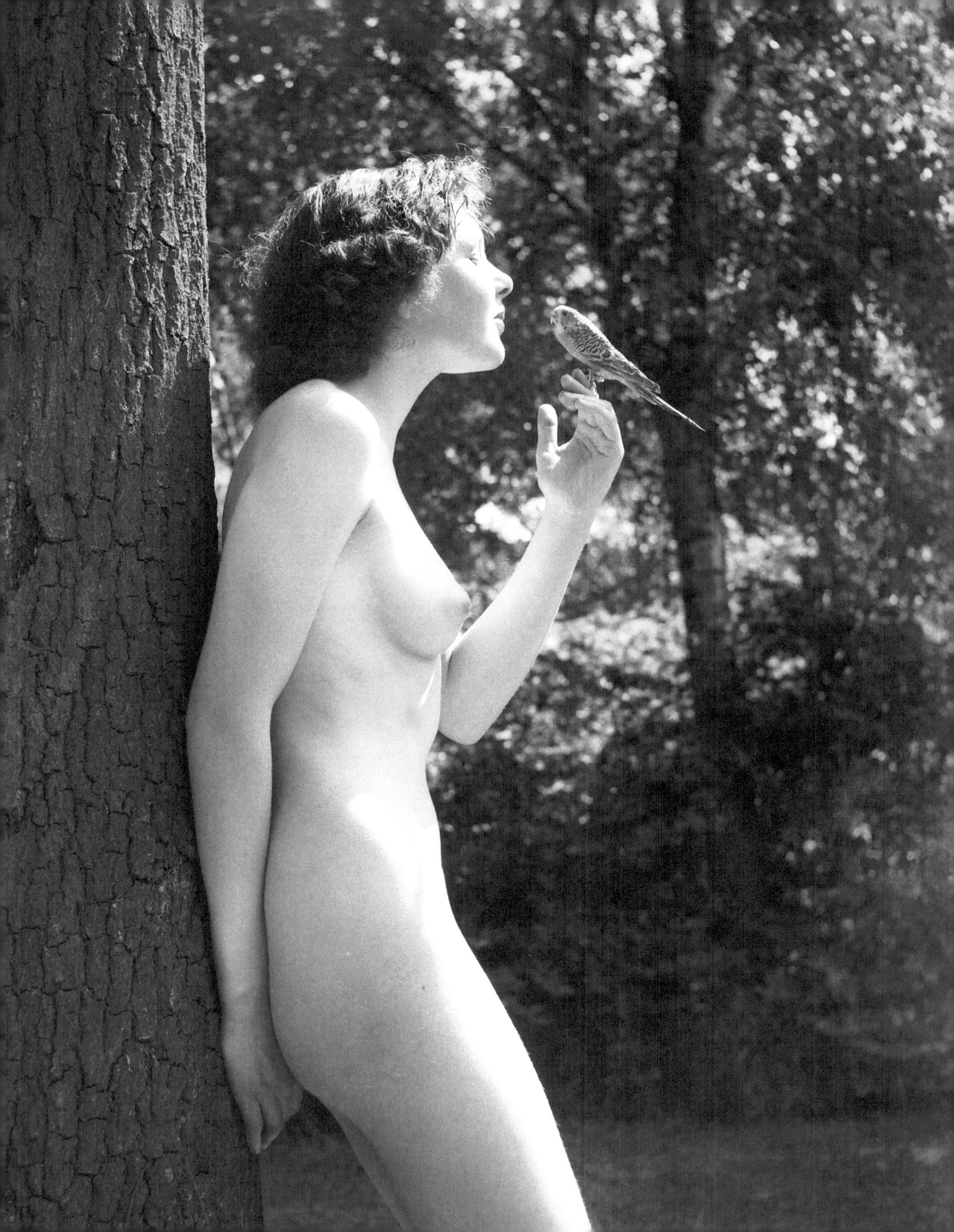

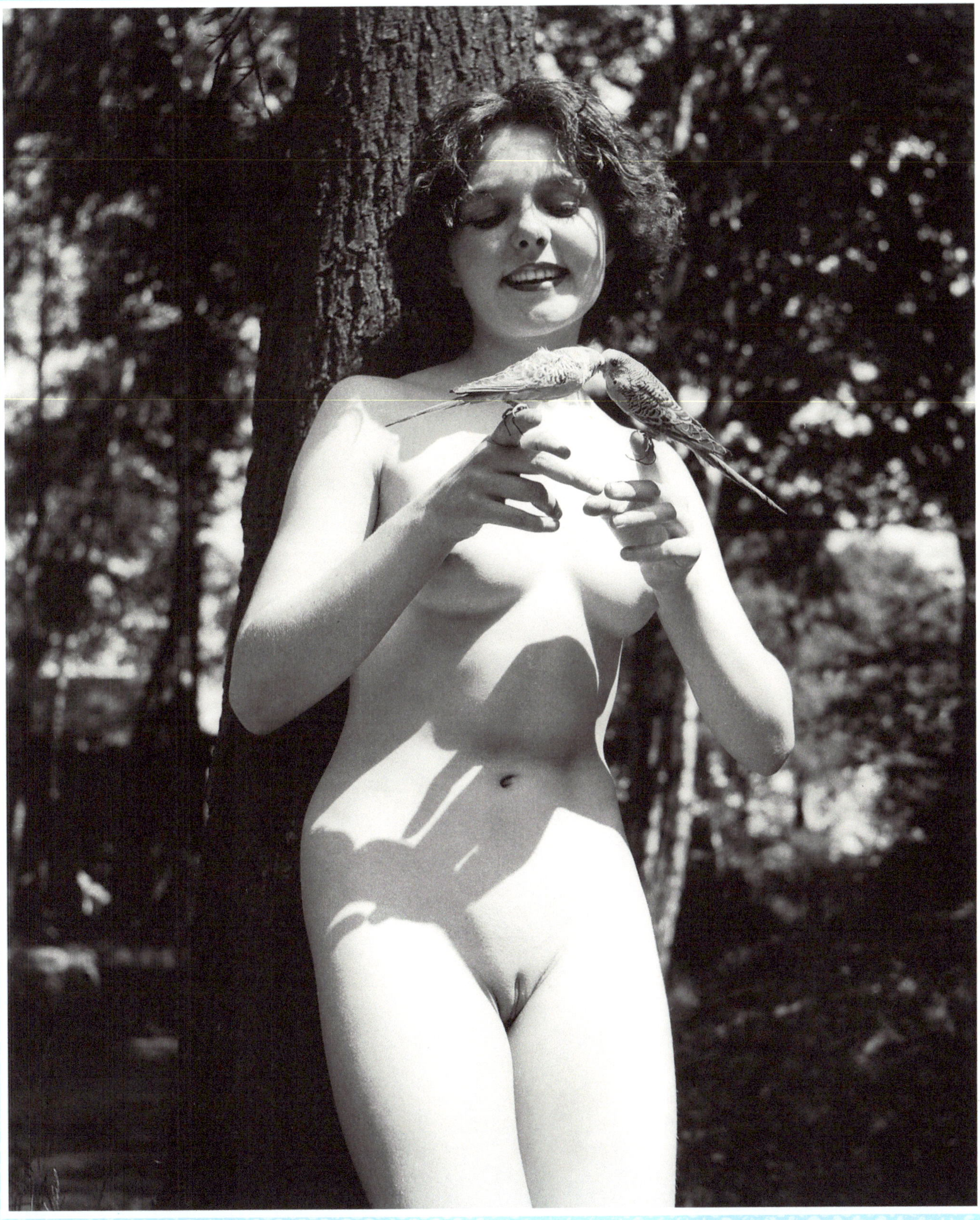

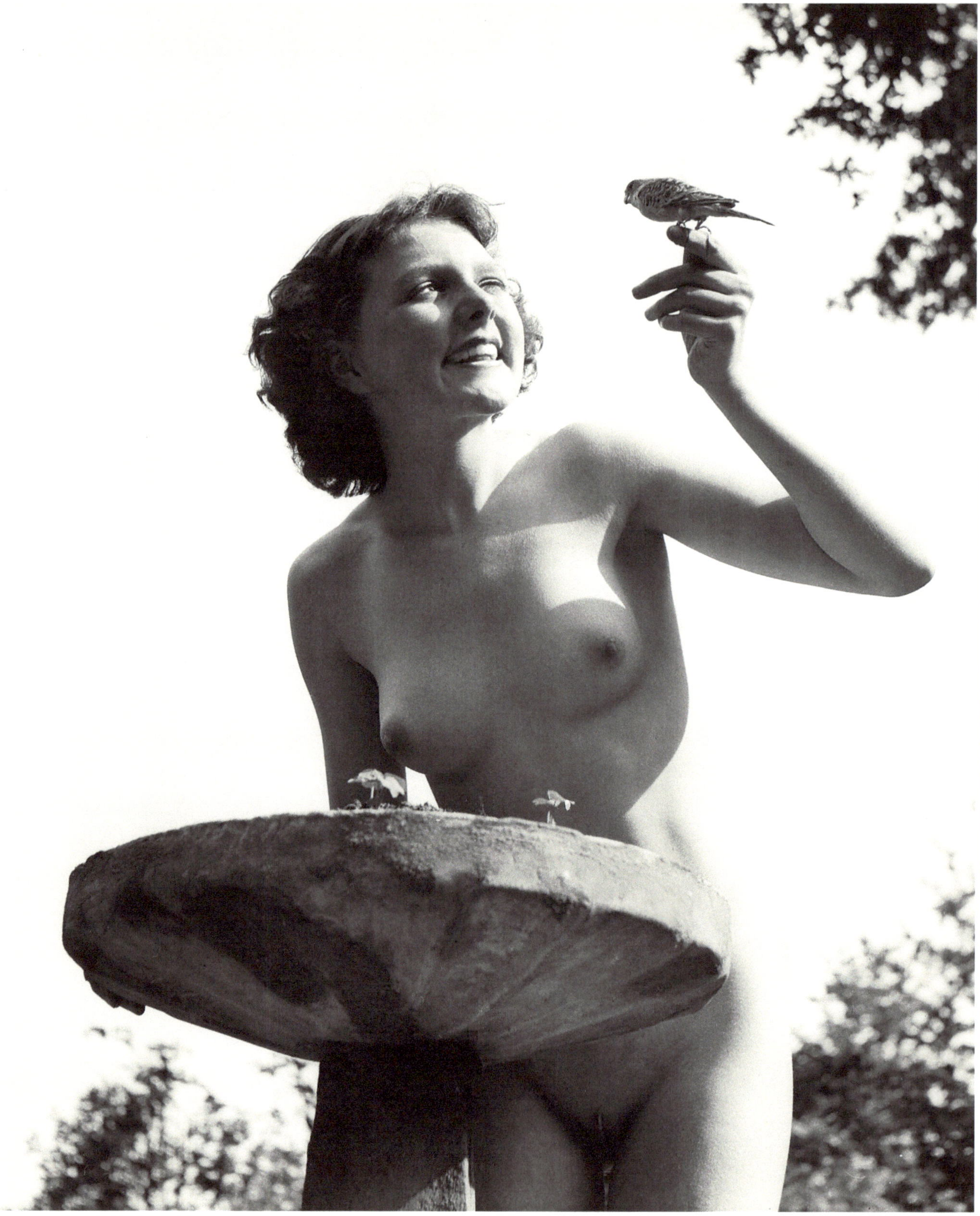

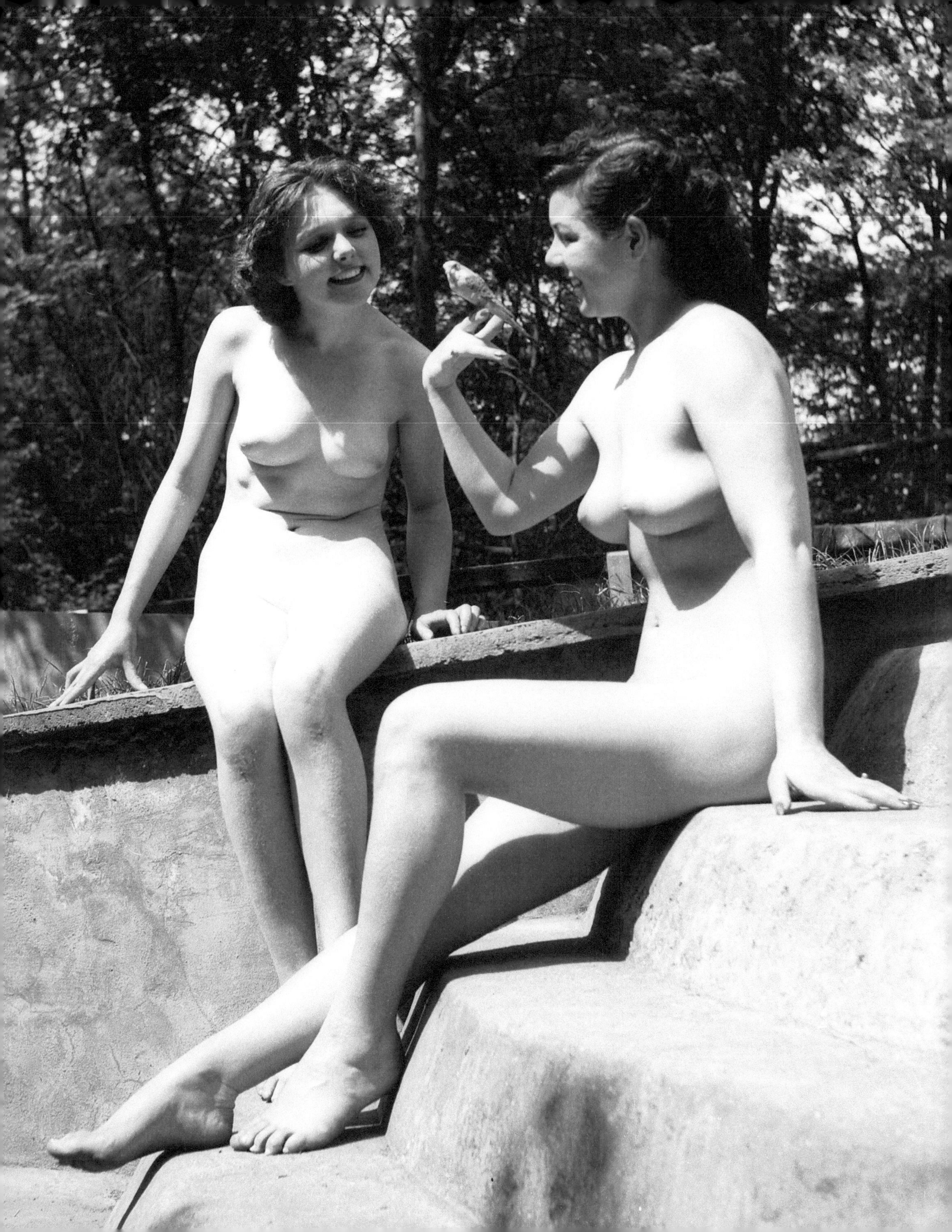

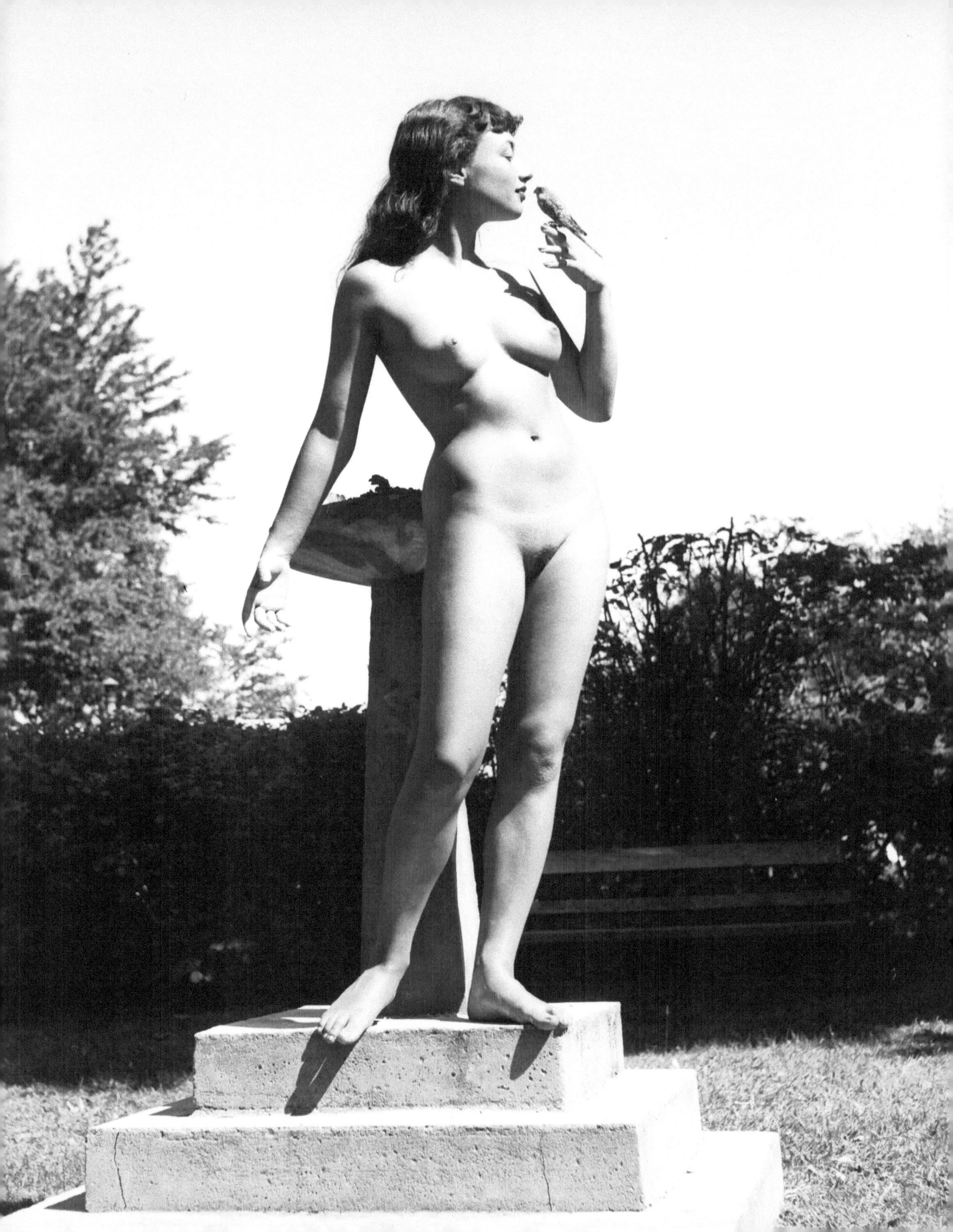

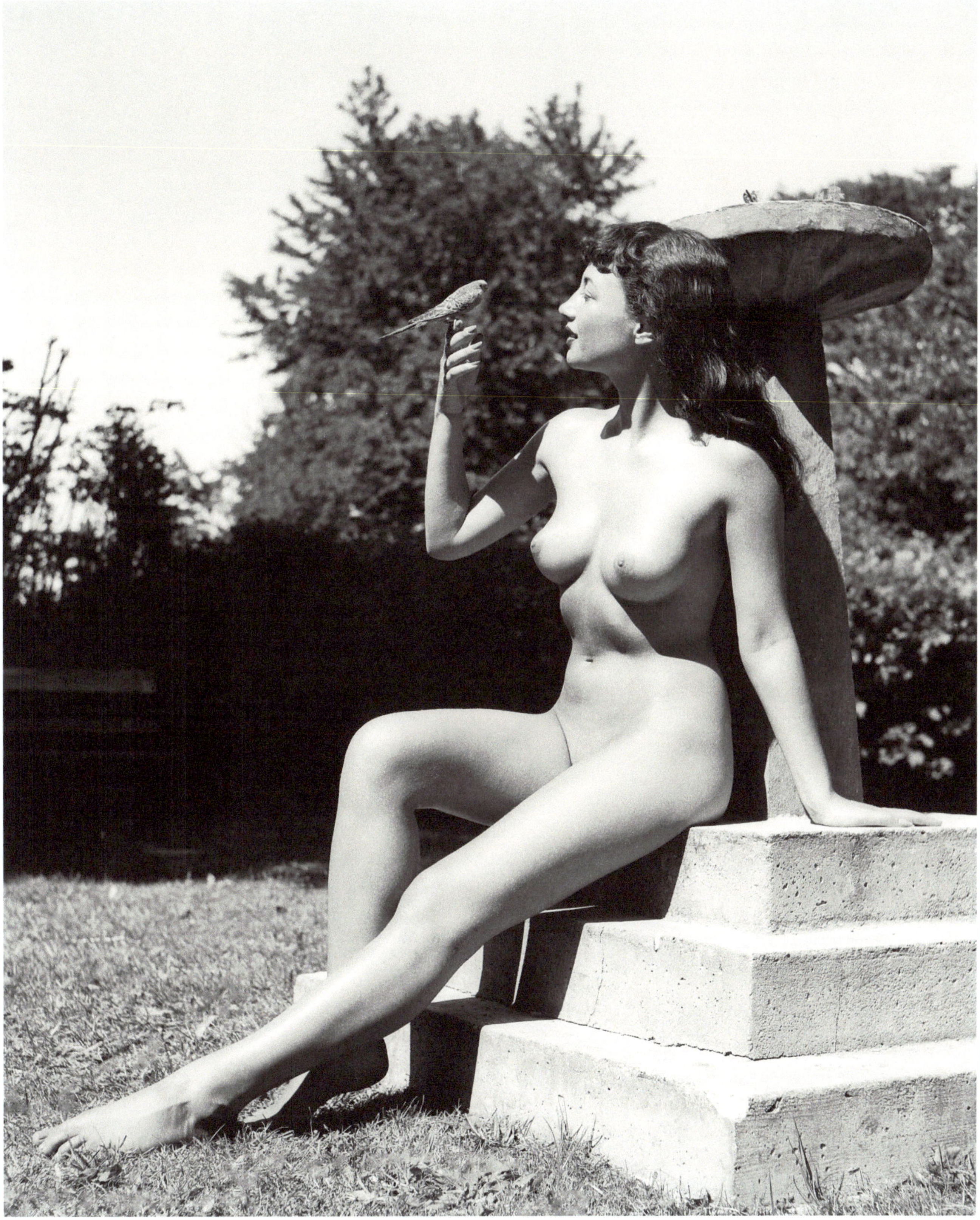

Left and above: Pamela Green photographed by the sundial in Spielplatz naturist village in the early 1950s.

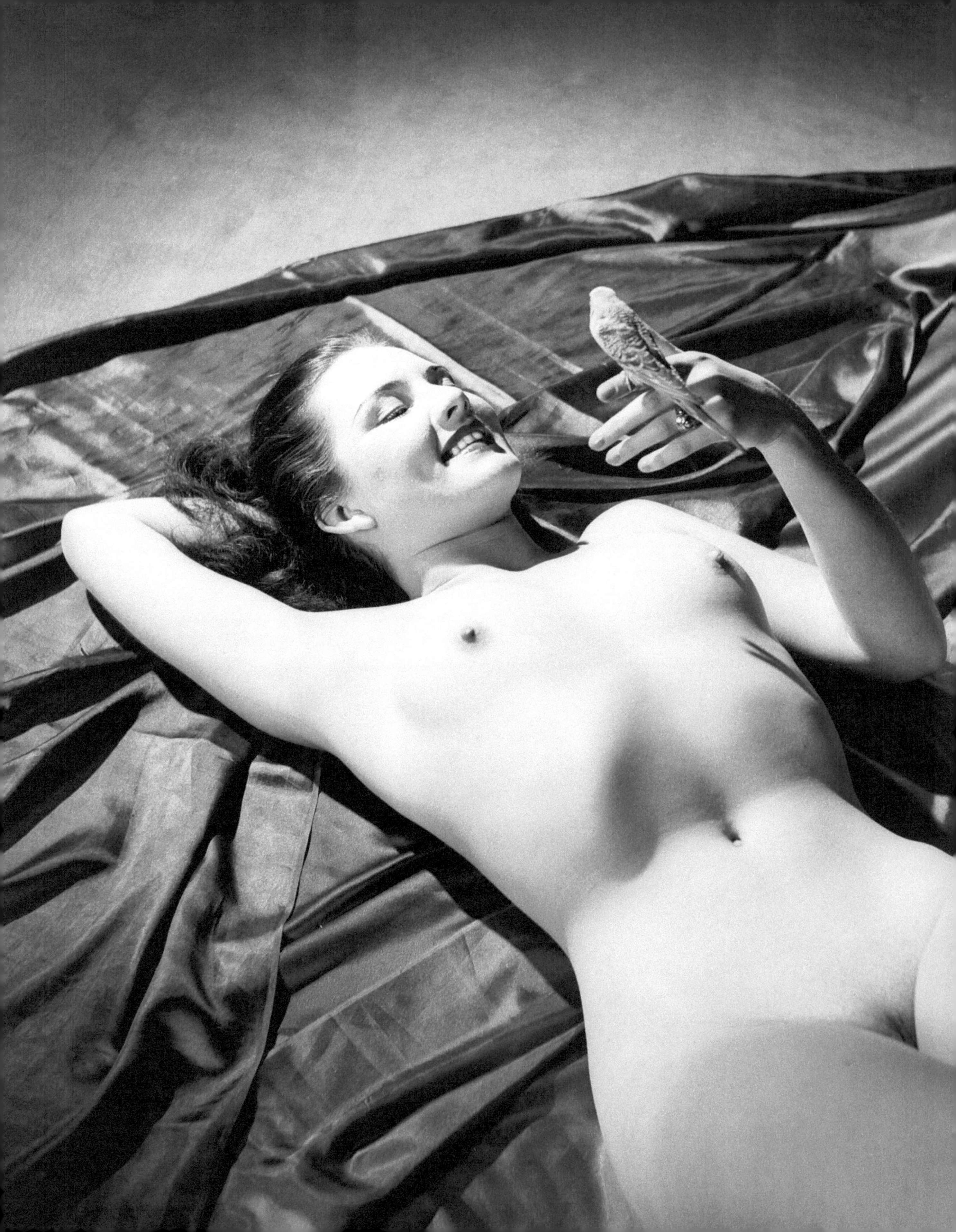

AVAILABLE TITLES FROM WOLFBAIT

Doing Rude Things
The history of the British sex film.

NEW! **Cinema au Naturel**
A history of nudist film.

Miniten: Rules of the Game
Invented in the 1930s, Miniten is a tennis-like game played by naturists.

Naked as Nature Intended
The epic tale of a nudist picture by Pamela Green, with photographs by Douglas "Dambuster" Webb, DFM.

The Naked Truth About Harrison Marks
The notorious biography by Franklyn Wood.

Past Masters of the Nude
An illustrated bibliography of nude photography books published in England from 1896 to 1960.

THE STEPHEN GLASS COLLECTION

Amazons of Yesteryear
A rare, action-packed collection of images of wrestling women of the 1940s and 1950s.

Beauty Off-Duty
Relaxed, everyday moments caught on camera.

Naked in the Menagerie
A playful look at Eve accompanied by her animal friends.

Nudist Camp Follies – volumes 1 and 2
An intimate look at the natural and free atmosphere in Sun Clubs.

Nymphs and Naiads
Beauty unadorned and outdoors.

NEW! **Poise and Pose**
A magnificent series of photographs of female beauty taken in the studio.

Order online at wolfbait.co.uk

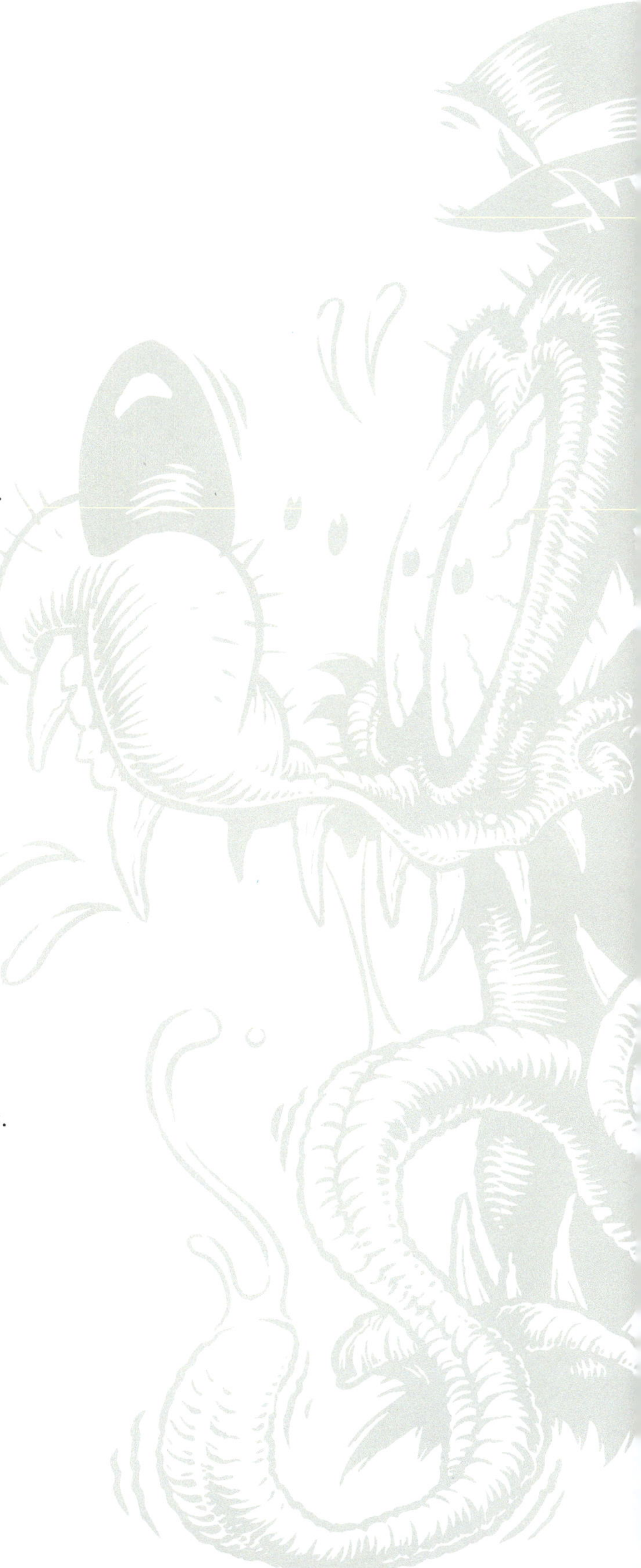

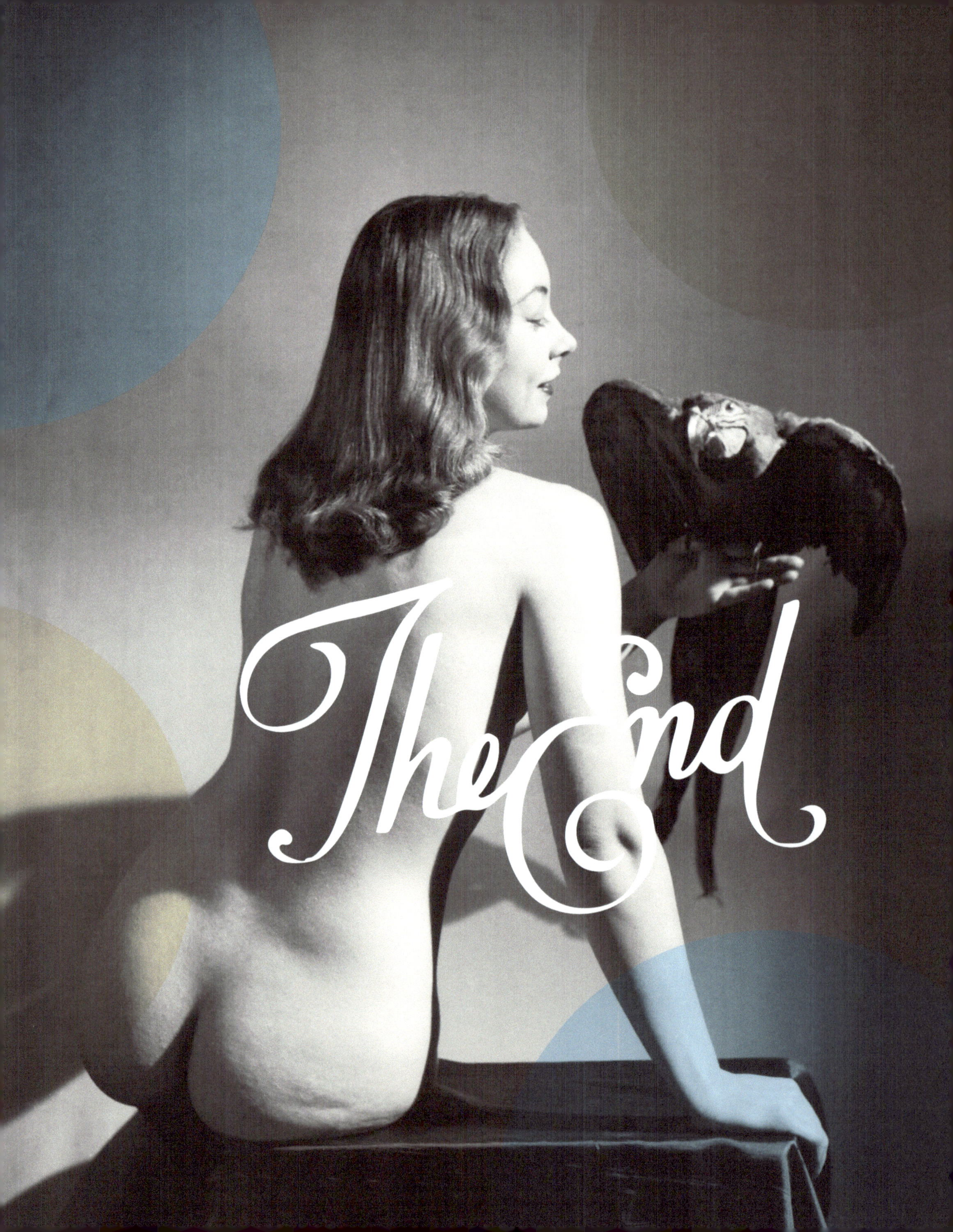
The End

www.ingramcontent.com/pod-product-compliance
Ingram Content Group UK Ltd.
Pitfield, Milton Keynes, MK11 3LW, UK
UKHW061034310726
14089UKWH00010B/232
9781999744175